We Power:

Building Powerful Relationships That Can Change Your Work and the World

Anderson W. Williams

For Charlie and Zoe: may you always know the power of being sisters, and the power of we in whatever you do.

Acknowledgments

Powerful relationships are the kind you can trust an extremely rough first draft of a book to when you can no longer see it critically yourself. A special thank you to those who willingly took a mess of my thinking and still worked through it to give me invaluable feedback: Michael Burcham, Terry Pickeral, Rich Games, Teri Dary, Bill Hughes, Elandria Williams, and my brother Charlie Williams. Thanks for trusting me enough to know I would listen to feedback and could make something of the mess I shared with you. Additional thanks to Michael Burcham for not only working through that first draft but also having faith enough to stick with me through successive drafts and conversations, helping make this book better and my thinking clearer along the way. Thanks to my family - Mom, Charlie Joe, Annie B., Melissa, Cora, Olivia, my wife Katie and daughters Charlie and Zoe - for making me want to be better and do more in the time I have here.

TABLE OF CONTENTS

About This Book

Power is a function of every human relationship. It is a dynamic between and among people and institutions. Power colors and informs the way we see and experience the world in the tiniest of ways and in the most systemic of ways.

Too many books, trainings, and related guides to leadership, taking action, empowering ourselves, or organizing with others for social change assume that we see, recognize, and accept our own power. In reality, most of us enter the fray of social, organizational, political, or other advocacy and change work deeply unsure of our power – perhaps even wholly unaware of the role power plays in our lives, relationships, and work. So, when we meet the inevitable challenges, make the necessary mistakes, and face the certain defeats, we often accept these setbacks as validation of our own lack of power, and thus a validation of the perceived power of others. Not only is this response self-defeating, but it serves and sustains the status quo. When we don't understand power, we are easy to control by those who do.

This is not a book that intends to teach you how to lead or to organize or create policy change in your organization or your community. It is a book that aspires to help you see yourself, others, and your work through the prism of power. It will guide you toward building the relationships you need, creating strategies that align with those relationships, and putting both into action to positively impact your work and the world. To make this happen, we must be informed by a deeper understanding of the overt and covert power structures and dynamics that surround us. After all, we can't transform power if we don't first understand it.

Opening

Years ago, I had the opportunity to spend a couple of days doing some training and consulting work with Special Olympics Arizona. Part of my work was to help a team of youth and adults in a program called Project UNIFY refocus and reground their work. They were part of a state and national effort advocating and modeling inclusive schools, where students with and without intellectual disabilities sat side-by-side in classrooms and played side-by-side in inclusive sports. They were trying to figure out how to take their work to the next level, to get more schools and more community partners involved. After some early successes, youth and staff turnover had left them feeling a bit rudderless.

The kind of visioning and planning I facilitated among the team began personal and individual and built from there toward the work they were trying to accomplish together. They knew that they not only needed to live the values of inclusion internally among themselves, but they needed to be able to speak to them, to evangelize, to bring others into the work. They needed to find the power in their disabilities and the power in their abilities and help others do the same.

I started the initial meeting by simply asking everyone what personal values being a part of this work helped them live out. Why was the work so important to them? We went around the room and, of course, I was inspired by the sense of love and friendship and equity and justice articulated by the teens as well as the commitment of the adult staff to those same ideals. Many spoke of their experiences being ostracized and bullied because of their disability. They didn't want others to have to go through that. Others spoke of having siblings with disabilities. They wanted to share

11

with others the love and respect they had for their brothers and sisters. Still others talked about how transformative their friendships among youth with and without disabilities had been to them and their understanding of themselves, their school, and the broader world. They believed they could change the world based on these relationships. For a facilitator, this was clearly fertile ground.

I got a little concerned, however, as one young woman with intellectual disabilities who had been quite vocal up to this point, prior to this specific question about values, had not yet responded to my prompt. So, I stopped and explicitly, but gently, asked if she had anything she would like to share. Without a verbal response, she dropped her head and began writing, slowly and deliberately.

The room was silent. She kept writing, slowly, deliberately.

(How long do I give her? I have never worked with this young woman. This could go on for hours for all I know!)

She kept writing, slowly, deliberately.

(Are any of the other youth giving me an idea that it's time to move ahead? What about the adults? Should I move on and come back to her? We really don't have that much time!)

No cues. The rest of the team was quiet and patiently waiting. So, I sat down and did the same.

I tried not to watch her for fear of her feeling any sort of pressure to hurry, but she was in a zone and really working with her thoughts. It probably wouldn't have mattered. She kept writing. As she approached the end of the first page of notes, I again began to wonder just how long this could or should last. But, I waited.

Finally, at the end of page one, she lifted her head. She started to speak and then got timid and lost her thoughts. Her previous confidence was gone. She was nervous, seemed a bit confused. Her friend, also from her high school, softly reminded her to look at the notes she had just written.

"Oh yeah." She picked up her pad and began to read. She read her own words on how much she valued friendship and sports and about how it helped organize her days (which was a very clear way she processed and understood the world, by her weekly calendar). She talked a bit about unified flag football (athletes with and without disabilities on the same teams); it was her first season to play.

And then, after a small pause, she said something profound: "Project UNIFY is an action thing to do and includes students and teachers and other people." Project UNIFY is "an action thing to do." Project UNIFY involves everyone in her school. Now, this may not seem like much, but she pretty much nailed it. Project UNIFY wasn't just about her participating, or having something to do with her time, not an activity but an action. It wasn't just about her or even her friends. It was about her school community and everyone who makes it up. It was about those relationships. Project UNIFY wasn't just about playing games or having fun like so many people may consider it. Working with peers and adults across physical and intellectual abilities was leading. It was modeling inclusion. It was social action, advocacy.

The rest of us had not spurred this kind of values discussion with our responses. Prior to her statement, which was longer and deeper than my one line here, the group was still kind of stumbling through the opening discussion of our meeting; the teens without intellectual disabilities still seeming a bit awkward talking about values. Then, this young woman blew the doors open and launched the team into talking about and being part of something bigger than ourselves, and yet still deeply personal.

Her words were not the only example of power in this story. In fact, her words really aren't even the point of my sharing the story. I share this story because of what happened in that room that day, and what didn't happen. The action/inaction of her peers in giving her the space to find and express her power was the critical lesson. It wasn't altruism. It wasn't just being nice. It was smart and strategic and their work was better for it. They were all more powerful because of the time and space they had allowed for her power to surface.

This young woman's insight and the subsequent discussion may never have happened in the pace and noise of our usual way of doing business or leading meetings or facilitating workshops. It wouldn't have had the space and time to surface if we were just "getting shit done" or "making it happen." We can't always make things happen. Sometimes we have to create the space to allow them to happen with and through others. And, this is the crux of the story: we lead by surfacing and exposing power, not merely deploying it; by sharing and growing power, not by claiming it.

How many times have we been in a business meeting or community meeting when there were two or three good minutes of unprompted silent thinking? When no one snickered nervously? Looked around? At their watch? Checked their phone? When people sat in the presence and fullness of silence?

14

When was the last time we were working on a new product or strategy or anything in a group when our opinion was so valued that our peers were willing to sit silently until we could formulate our thoughts? However long it took!? Even if we had to write a full page of notes first?

And yet, silence is part of what helped surface this young woman's power and voice. It didn't give them to her. She had them. We had to value her and each other enough to shut up, be patient, and let it happen. After all, it was our silent support that gave her a chance to process and express her world with the skills that she had, not based on the rules and skills of everyone else in the room.

If the young people and adults sitting around that table had been what we typically, mistakenly, call powerful leaders, we would have jumped into the silence and directed the young woman toward a response. We would have usurped her innate power, forcing it into our time and space needs. In other words, any of us could have intervened in the process to help deliver an "answer" or response that met our narrow definitions of power or voice – and in a timeframe that better suited our needs. We could have gotten her to say "The work is important because of my friends." And, we could have felt good about it. We could have checked it off the list. We could have celebrated the illusion of her voice and power and simultaneously claimed it, adding to our own. We could have said: Yes! Friends! Isn't that great? See how we engage students with intellectual disabilities? See what powerful leaders we are? And, it wouldn't have been her real answer. It would have been our answer.

We can often point at powerful leadership immediately. (Did you see that!? Did you see what he did? She said?) We often only understand powerful relationships with time and reflection (wow, what happened there? Or, how did that happen?). I, for one, didn't understand the power of that moment until days later when I was summarizing the experience as part of my reporting. Clearly, I'm still reflecting on it years later. What exactly happened there?

PART I:
Power

Our deepest fear is not that we are inadequate. Our deepest fear is that we are powerful beyond measure. It is our light, not our darkness that most frightens us. We ask ourselves, 'Who am I to be brilliant, gorgeous, talented, fabulous?' Actually, who are you not to be?...Your playing small does not serve the world. There is nothing enlightened about shrinking so that other people won't feel insecure around you. We are all meant to shine, as children do...And as we let our own light shine, we unconsciously give other people permission to do the same. As we are liberated from our own fear, our presence automatically liberates others.

- Marianne Williamson

The Challenges of Talking About Power

Power has no centre. It flourishes and reproduces itself in the patterns of the most ordinary interactions between people, the most taken-for-granted conversations, the shape of buildings and the layout of rooms, the convention about who sits where at the dinner table.[1]

- Howard Sercombe

Half of your master of power comes from what you do not do, what you do not allow yourself to get dragged into.[2]

– Robert Greene

Talking about power is extremely difficult. And yet, understanding power, perhaps even just being aware of it, is critical and the most potentially transformative condition of any relationship, to ourselves, to each other, to institutions, to the world around us. Power is like gravity: it affects us in every way, organizes how we live our lives, how we create, and how we orient to objects and others. Like gravity, power is so ubiquitous that it goes unnoticed, taken-for-granted, until it hurts us that is. (If it always helps, we call that privilege, which I will discuss later.)

So, if power is so important, so pervasive, why is it so difficult to talk about? It's not like we don't have the words we need, right?

In fact, there are too many words we use as a proxy for power that all get conflated with and confuse the core concept. This is the first reason power is so difficult to talk about: power itself is neutral, but its manifestations

---

[1] Sercombe, Howard. *Youth work ethics*. London: SAGE, 2010. 124 Print.
[2] Greene, Robert, and Joost Elffers. *The 48 Laws of Power*. London: Profile Ltd., 2010: xxi. Print.

and the words we use to describe them rarely are. Bertrand Russell in *Power: A New Social Analysis* defines power quite blandly as "the production of intended effects." There's not much offensive there. But, the concept of "intended effects" is actually extraordinarily complicated in the world of human affairs. As a result, there are myriad terms that describe both the positive and negative intended effects of power, and thereby convolute our understanding of the source concept. Strength, force, coercion, ability, faculty, authority, influence, dominance, mastery, control, – and a seemingly endless list of others. What do these things look like? Are they good or bad? For whom? Our response to all of these terms and our conflations of the various forms of power result directly from our personal experiences. We know power based on how we feel it and with what words we have to describe the experience of it. The effects, intended or not, therefore are infinitely muddled by our varying perspectives and interpretations, which themselves can change over time.

Imagine how confusing, and negative, our relationship to gravity would be if, rather than calling it gravity, we only used words like heaviness, pressure, weight, force, crushing, falling, dropping, collapsing and so on. Like power, if we relate to it merely as a narrow contextual experience, we lose its meaning in false simplicity and never reach a deeper understanding from which we can grow, evolve, and adapt. The more we point at power and talk about it critically, the more its complexities and entanglements in our lives will surface, and the more opportunity we will have to understand and use power in purposeful and meaningful ways. Alternately, the longer power remains over-simplified or unnamed, the more insidious it can become.

Thinking critically about seemingly simple topics or daily rote processes is the key to peeling back the layers of confusion and misunderstanding wrapped around power. For example, discipline is one power proxy that, if we stop and consider more critically, is a convoluted and potentially contradictory value that's a part of all of our individual, social, and institutional lives. The word discipline is ubiquitous in education, for example. I have spent countless hours in schools and community meetings focused on dropout prevention and other youth-related issues where the need for more discipline is invoked. Teachers say students need more discipline. Parents agree. The police show up for severe disciplinary infractions. Resource officers and principals discipline students who get out of line. Students need the discipline to sit in their chairs and listen for hours on end. Discipline should be more strict; students say less strict. We have a discipline problem in schools. Everyone agrees.

But, as this varying list of uses suggests, discipline is a form of power with often contradictory implications and manifestations – despite our perceived agreement on the topic. Discipline in schools, and as well as in the workplace, is something that gets doled out to those who need it, those who step out of line, transgress the rules. It is external to the recipient - the disciplined. It is a tool of structures and organizations to try and manage and control behavior that falls below a certain acceptable threshold. It is a necessary organizational tool – even if its distribution is criminally unequal based on other forms of power that I talk about in this book. (African-American boys, for example, are dramatically more likely to be disciplined in schools.) Discipline, if equitably applied, serves as a tool of the social contract of a society or organization. We agree to these rules and norms in exchange for some perceived benefit, so we also agree when someone breaks them that they deserve to be disciplined. Regardless, discipline of this kind is power as enforcement, control, and authority externally derived from the disciplined. Again, it is neither implicitly negative nor positive.

The discipline, on the other hand, that could actually solve the high school dropout crisis, heal toxic organizational cultures, or transform other social ills is a discipline of a very different nature. It is not a tool of top-down, structural control, but of self-control. Internal, self-discipline also supports the social contract of a civil society, but in much more fundamental and sustainable ways. Self-discipline is internally sourced and driven. It is not imposed. It cannot be imposed. It is evoked and developed through relationships and experiences, through self-reflection, and a sense of purpose. Instead of talking endlessly about the need to discipline students or employees or anyone else purely from an external locus of control, we should invest in the environments and experiences and resources that will help cultivate discipline sourced from an internal locus of control. In a distinction I will use throughout this book, this is the difference between *transactional* discipline and *transformational* discipline; the former imposes power, that latter cultivates it.

So, basically, discipline does not equal discipline, no matter how many times we say it in meetings and share our opinions on it, and nod our heads thinking we are in agreement. And, this muddying of concepts mirrors the challenge we face with understanding power more broadly: if we don't acknowledge it, critique it, and define what we really mean, in specific contexts, with specific people, many of our most important conversations and our most well-intended work will prove counterproductive. Our work will get mired in the murkiness of ill-defined power relations that ultimately will undermine the power of our work.

Unfortunately, we often don't realize this fact until it's too late to do much about it, which brings us to the second reason power is so difficult to talk about: power itself is invisible. It "has no centre." Most of what we observe is at least one step removed from the source of power itself. We see and describe the results or even the symptoms of a powerful action. We see and invoke discipline, for example, but not our potentially contradictory interpretations of power that underlie it or define it for us. We don't evaluate the power dynamics that led to the behavior that required the discipline, so we also never truly understand the success or failures of the forms of discipline imposed to address it.

To complicate things further, power is both action and inaction, the act and the non-act. Consider the nonviolent Civil Rights Movement, for example. The power of the segregationist State and of Jim Crow was manifest in fire hoses, German Shepherds, bully clubs, beatings, handcuffs, and arrests. Their power was authority. Their power was control. Their power was both overt and covert state-sponsored action. Power (and powerlessness) was inscribed in the law, defended by the State with all necessary force. This is the power segregationists were certain would break the nonviolent, youthful opposition, and put the perceived powerless young revolutionaries back in their structurally powerless place.

These nonviolent protestors were not powerless, however. The young people who boycotted businesses, marched in silence, and sat-in at lunch counters were demonstrating power as a sort of inaction, or non-event. To be clear, marches, sit-ins, and boycotts were all actions; that is not my point. These nonviolent resistance strategies were very carefully coordinated, externally and internally disciplined actions. But, their power came from what didn't happen. Their power was that they were non-events within the State's definition and deployment of power. They redefined power in terms of peace, love, and moral abstention from violence. They transformed it. This was their counterforce. These were children. Black children. Everyone knew they had no power. That's why they had such power.

If this seems confusing or perhaps convoluted, just imagine if, at one sit-in at the lunch counters in downtown Nashville, just one of the young students had finally had enough abuse, and decided to strike back in-kind. Imagine if just one of those students had thrown a punch at their white antagonists and abusers; imagine if they had pulled out their own hidden bully club. Imagine if just one had violently resisted arrest. Imagine how that would have changed the narrative and the power of their moral movement. I don't want to simplify things, but I believe the movement, and the country for that matter, would be very different. Certainly, my own city of Nashville would be a different place.

These young leaders were appealing to, and using, a higher power than those of the segregationist's social and cultural institutions and laws. It was a power that tapped into the moral core of individuals inside and outside the movement and took a longer, historical view of the work of winning equal rights for all. As King stated and thus defined their work: "The arc of the moral universe is long, but it bends toward justice." And, herein lies yet another reason power is difficult to talk about: it's not one thing, but a dynamic between and among people and institutions and social, political, and economic systems, over time and in places. Power is a function of all relationships. Power is rarely experienced as truly equal, and, in fact, rarely is. How power inequalities manifest themselves and how they are interpreted in the context of the relationship, time, place, and work will color any sort of good/bad or other value statement on that power, relationship, or work.

Howard Sercombe in *Youth Work Ethics* provides needed clarity and insight: *"For some commentators…all relations which involve power differentials are, by definition, oppressive and unjust. I don't think this helps us very much, though. Social life inevitably generates power differentials, whether recognised or not. Any division of labor will move power towards some people and away from others. There are no communities without power processes, at least at the informal level of popularity, influence and differential respect. Wherever a relationship is mobilised for some kind of joint action, you have a power relation."*[3] Power is a fact of human relations, and equal power is not always the goal or the conceivable reality in most situations or relationships.

Understanding and interpreting power as a relational dynamic helps us better understand our relationships and our world in the present and where we hope to take them in the future. To do this well, however, also requires a deeper critical analysis of where we have been. This is perhaps the primary reason power is so uncomfortable for many people to talk about: a historical reinterpretation of power undermines much of what we

---

[3] Sercombe, Howard. *Youth work ethics*. London: SAGE, 2010. 122-3 Print.

know and understand of the human story. It shakes some pretty serious foundations of identity, race, regionalism, nationalism and much more. The narrative of these foundations has been told by the powerful. The conquerors. The victors. The pugilists. The telling and owning by themselves and acceptance by others of this historical power narrative is both an example of and a source of their continued power in the present.

These powerful few (mostly white, heterosexual, Euro-centric, Christian, males) have written a narrative that serves as a self-reinforcing loop, a self-fulfilling prophecy of power. For this reason, talking about power, in and of itself, can be seen as transgressive to our historical norms. Talking about power as something to be shared and something implicit to all human beings is definitively transgressive to these norms. A highly controlled and narrowly cultivated narrative of power has ensured that the attributes most closely related to those in control of systems and institutions are those deemed powerful, that the positions they hold are those of power. Again, it's a self-reinforcing loop. To understand how this happens (not in historical context but in an understanding of power itself), we must explore power as both human construct and condition.

Power as Construct

Power doesn't corrupt people; people corrupt power.
                                            - William Gaddis

Power as a construct is the form of power we are most familiar with, the one we recognize and name as power. As I've discussed, we typically construct the story of power through a very specific, and very narrow lens, one reflective of our society, values, and social norms. In capitalist societies, for example, we tell it through the lens of competition. Us versus them. We tell the story of power through the triumph of the victor and the defeat of the other. Something either claimed or lost. We treat it as zero sum.

Such simplified constructs of power narrow the concept to a degree that makes it seemingly easy to understand without really having to think too hard. On the other hand, when we aren't thinking too hard or working to construct new power dynamics, we by default are accepting the ones that are already in place. In his best-selling book *The 48 Laws of Power*, Robert Greene scans and distills 3000 years of human history into a set of laws of power with historical examples of their application. The book is huge and feels comprehensive. I found it deeply unsettling, if illuminating. It tells a distressing history of people and culture – albeit a seemingly accurate one – that surfaces the repeated patterns of power that define that history. These distilled laws of power reinforce the story of the historical winners and losers, and the forms of power that made them so. The book is rife with words like enemy, manipulation, defeat, impress, intimidate, conquer and so many more. It tells story after story of the vanquishing and the vanquished. Here is a sampling of the laws:

Law: Get others to do the work for you, but always take the credit.

Law: Learn to keep people dependent on you.

Law: Court attention at all costs.

Law: Conceal your intentions.

Law: Use selective honesty and generosity to disarm your victim.

Law: Pose as a friend, work as a spy.

Law: Keep others in suspended terror: cultivate an air of unpredictability.

Law: Crush your enemy totally.

All of the laws aren't this grotesque, but there are far more of this ilk than that of the power I am advocating here.

Don't get me wrong. I get it. Read history, Shakespeare, or even watch what's on TV tonight and we can see how obsessed we are with this type of power. Again, these laws, and sadly much of human history according to Greene's work, represent a construct of power that not only protects and reinforces existing power structures but also simplifies the concept into a dyad, those with and without, power claimed, stolen, expressed, suppressed. And, perhaps this is the most distressing thing about our human understanding of power: it is miniscule compared to our actual relationship to and interactions with it. Nothing that is a function of human relationships is as simple as a dyad, no matter how many stories we tell ourselves and no matter how comfortable we allow ourselves to be with such false simplicity.

Can you imagine, for example, if we defined other dynamics of human relationships with such simplicity? What if we accepted love in such narrow and dogmatic terms? What if we only understood love in terms of love expressed or love vanquished? What if we ignored how love grows and changes and evolves over time? That we can fall in love and out of love? That time and age and circumstance matter? That love shared has the power to grow more love? That we can love children and partners and parents and friends in dramatically different ways? If we accepted love like we do power - as dyadic and zero sum - then my love for my children, for example, would take away from my capacity to love my wife, when it actually grows it. My love for my family would consume a finite resource that I could otherwise share with my friends. If we understood love like we do power, we would lose the nuance of our social and emotional selves. We would lose access to and exploration of what it means to be human.

And yet, love is an expression of power. In *On Secrets, Lies, and Silence*, the poet Adrienne Rich describes love as the power to break out of narrow and false constructs that we apply to ourselves and to the world around us. *"An honorable human relationship — that is, one in which two people have the right to use the word "love" — is a process, delicate, violent, often terrifying to both persons involved, a process of refining the truths they can tell each other. It is important to do this because it breaks down human self-delusion and isolation. It is important to do this because in doing so we do justice to our own complexity. It is important to do this because we can count on so few people to go that hard way with us."*

Rich is showing us how love can be the power that moves us beyond our own self-constructed limitations and our own oversimplification of our humanity. She is articulating love as an implicit, internal power that is greater than the arbitrary, external constructions of power we encounter every day. Love lives outside of those constructs, within us, and is what connects us to each other. She highlights how external power constructs help us simplify and navigate a complex world but can also leave us feeling isolated.

In some cases, these simplified delusions of power are a matter of survival. The world is too big and too dynamic to process all at once and all the time. We find safety in simplifying our world and deferring our own power to it. However, we too often forget that we made this choice; that we are the ones who initially create such limiting constructs relinquishing our responsibility. In time then, we allow ourselves to be burdened by these very constructs long after they've lost utility and start to become constraints. We are the creators of our own powerlessness.

I first became aware of this process as I traversed adolescence and into early adulthood and wrestled with Religion as it had been presented to me via the Christian Church. I came from a Religious family, a family of revival and street corner preachers, of startup Nazarene churches. At birth, I was Dedicated into the Nazarene Church. We went to the Church of Christ for years, where I also went to pre-school. I went to a Catholic

30

elementary school and diligently memorized my catechism, learned and practiced the rituals of first communion and confession even though I was denied those sacraments because I was a Protestant. I sat alone in the back of the church in second grade when the time came for my peers' souls to be saved. I was going to hell because I wasn't Catholic. As a teen, I was Confirmed into the Methodist Church, so I did all of the due diligence around their version of that sacrament. For years around that time, I sat listening to 19th century Methodist hymns droning and echoing through neo-gothic architecture. Far from awe inspiring or spiritually uplifting, the methodical chanting inspired adolescent cynicism. Why am I here? Is this really the sound of the moved human spirit? The enlightened? Do I really have to sit here and listen and recite someone else's words to pave my pathway to god? Surely, my connection to a higher power should feel more alive than this!

For years, I worked through this challenge internally and in discussions with peers and teachers and anyone else who would engage. At some point, however, I realized that my angst and confusion were due to my sense of being beholden to the Church for my access to god, beholden to a human construct, admittedly one that works for literally billions of people, but didn't for me. I realized the power to know and relate to god was within me and not controlled by any external construct. The Church was not a singular construct anyway, right? If it were, how could I be a Church of Christ-Nazarene-Catholic-Methodist?

While this is perhaps a controversial personal angle to share, I believe people have the choice to do what works for them to cultivate their own spiritual lives. The lessons of my own power that surfaced through these

31

years of confusion and effort changed my life and my work - not just my relationship to god - in every way. I found my locus of control, the source of my liberation deep within me, my access to a higher power independent of others or their power constructs.

A decade later, working in and around public education, I observed a similar institutionalized, secular form of deference to construct over individual power. Over a hundred years ago, we designed a system of education for a variety of reasons and for a social and economic context that has nothing to do with the ways we live and learn today. A hundred years ago, there were reasons we had formal desks in rows, classrooms organized by age, calendars organized by farming seasons, and curricula delivered by a central authoritative figure. Today, everything we know about how the brain develops and how learning happens with young people is actually in direct contradiction to this century-old model. Additionally, the context for this model and how it fits into our lives, social habits, and economy has totally changed. We don't live in an agrarian society. Access to information is not merely the realm of adults, experts, or formal institutions. Our beliefs and understanding about discipline are different. The diversity of the communities served by schools is different. Our goals for students when they graduate are different. The list could go on and on.

And yet, here we are, in the 21st century, beholden to a model of education we know doesn't actually meet our needs. We are beholden to a defunct construct. We act as if the classroom with a teacher in front and kids in desks in rows with textbooks (even if digital) and worksheets and homework and so forth are all somehow a divine edict that we dare not upend, or don't have the power to upend. When in fact, it is a model we make and remake every single day with our choices and actions/inactions. A relative few leaders and schools (thousands for sure, but the scope of the issue is massive) are rebellious and innovative enough to nibble at the margins, to challenge the power of the system, but we know the whole system needs to be rethought. Most of us, however, either won't rethink it or don't have the courage or creativity to put our thoughts into action. We are trapped in a broken system of our own creating.

At a much smaller, perhaps more immediate level, we can even consider the daily work life of people who spend most of our jobs in a run-of-the-mill office setting. Few of us ask for more meetings, phone calls, or emails. Research suggests, in fact, that the overwhelming volume of these is what increases stress and burnout and actually impedes our productivity and innovation. And yet, most of us just accept it all as just part of the job – the construct of work. Most of us don't try to rethink the hows and whys of meetings without agendas, a clear purpose, and true time constraints. We don't upend the dozens of useless emails that frustrate and distract us from more meaningful work.

And, it's not just in companies. I have worked on numerous committees, volunteer groups, boards, and the like, with truly brilliant, intensely motivated, and incredibly powerful individuals. And, I've watched and felt as all of us over time ended up as less powerful than the sum of our parts, looking around at each other like we are sedated, wondering why we still come to these meetings, like we don't have something else to do with our time. We hold onto the sense of purpose that brought us together long after our poor process has largely usurped our power to affect that purpose.

Again, emails, meeting agendas, endless committee meetings and so forth may not feel like particularly potent topics in a book on power. However, just consider the volume and frequency of our interactions with those broken constructs and the daily stress it puts on us, the energy it usurps, how they trigger our disengagement. Surely, this demonstrates a power dynamic among people and processes in our work. All of these processes and interactions are controllable and changeable variables in our lives. We are choosing to maintain the status quo instead of making it better. We are deferring our power instead of putting it into action.

When I helped found Zeumo our goal was to make communication easier and better and less stressful for high school students and, in a later iteration, physicians. We designed a relatively simply mobile communication app for internal organizational communication that was supported by the tools and analytics you might find to manage external marketing campaigns. We believed we could be as purposeful and targeted in communicating with people we know, people in our communities, schools, hospitals, or other organizations, as a marketer is with millions of data points and strangers out on the internet. We believed we could communicate better and increase engagement of our people if we started with the right tools; and we went out to try and prove it. We didn't change the world, or education, or healthcare for that matter, but we also didn't pretend we were powerless to do something different.

Power of Privilege and Oppression

People's power to act, even as leaders, is always constrained by forces that are visible to them and those that are hidden, structured into circumstances of birth, race, class – or those that are banished from consciousness.[4]

– Amanda Sinclair

As I hope you can tell, the constructs of power can be large and small, from systemic to individual, from active, overt control to passive, covert sublimation. Over time, these power constructs, if not challenged, can become so frequent, so normalized and accepted, that they become structured into how we see and understand ourselves in the world. Structural privilege and oppression are the cumulative manifestations of unjust social, political, and economic constructions of power, the decisions and designs we make, remake, or reinforce through action or inaction as a society, at every level of interaction, every single day.

A full discussion of concepts of privilege and oppression is certainly beyond my purposes, or abilities, here. In fact, given my own privilege, any effort I might make to impart the experiences, mindsets, challenges or otherwise of the oppressed would be inherently dubious. But, it is critical here for us to see how concepts of privilege and oppression represent a meta-construct of power, created by man and imposed upon man – and thus, changeable by man.

We can look at privilege and oppression through a similar prism, as complicit forces with opposing results within the same construct. In doing so, we must first

---

[4] Sinclair, Amanda. *Leadership for the disillusioned: moving beyond myths and heroes to leading that liberates.* Crows Nest, N.S.W.: Allen & Unwin, 2007: 89. Print.

understand the nature of and relationship between the external version of the construct and the internal version. The power constructs I have discussed so far mostly focus on external systems, whether it is the segregationist State, education writ large, or office practices on a much smaller scale. These constructs inherently benefit some and negatively impact others. But, what happens over time is that each of us tends to adapt to the construct. We accept it as a fact of our external social, political, or economic life and then, over time, we internalize it as something within and of ourselves. Students at this school drop out, so why don't I? I don't learn or work this way, so I must be dumb or bad at my job. The standard of beauty is blond hair and blue eyes, so I must be ugly. The standard of strength is male so I must be weak.

Alternately, if I have access to quality educational, civic, or work related institutions, am blond haired and blue eyed, if I am male, if I am traditionally smart then the world of opportunity is served to me. The door starts open; I don't have to open it. The answer starts as yes; I don't have to prove myself. The assumption is that I am educated, informed, and trustworthy; so I don't always have to make my case. Over time, as I receive these messages, I too internalize them. Rather than marginalize me, they reinforce my sense of self and prove my position of power. My unjust privilege becomes my internalized supremacy.

If you haven't figured it out yet, I am male, have blond hair and blue eyes, and have always been considered smart. I am also heterosexual. I was raised as a Christian in its many forms, as I have discussed. My parents were educated. I am educated. I am the poster child of privilege. The difference for me in my life has been that I always knew I was privileged. I was fortunate to know at a very early age what privilege even was. My parents taught me and reminded me of my privilege every day when I had questions about other friends and neighbors, about homeless people I met on the street, about all of the people with all of the differences that surrounded me growing up.

I provide a bit more description, context and local color around my upbringing in *Creating Matters* that I won't repeat here. But, it was easy for me to see my privilege because I grew up privileged in a geographical island of poverty. The distinction was stark. I grew up as "the other" even though I was white. I was the bizarre child of privilege who never actually felt like he fit in. I was an "insider" by social, economic, and cultural construction and yet always felt like an outsider. So, in some form or fashion, I guess I have been wrestling with my privilege my whole life, fighting to make sure my privilege never became internalized.

The Lightness of Internalized Privilege

If naming privilege is the first step to preventing its potential for developing a sense of superiority or supremacy, understanding how and why we are privileged is the most critical. We have to see the structures and feel the structures to name the structures. But this presents the privilege conundrum: when we are privileged we don't really feel it. Privilege ensures things that are events for the unprivileged are non-events for us. Privilege means we aren't afraid when we are pulled over for a speeding ticket. Privilege means we don't get the extra scrutiny in a job application or interview, on a business loan. Privilege means we have choices and personal and professional opportunities that seem just a fact of our being. Privilege means we and others have assumptions for our success, presumptions about the high quality of our character. Privilege means we are in the norm, not different, not other. Privilege is the ultimate social, cultural, and economic non-event. So, there is little to make us acknowledge it, much less feel it.

If we are willing to reflect, however, or have had some experience with our privilege or with those less privileged that triggers some critical thought, there is actually a sort of unbearable lightness to privilege, one that ties my privilege implicitly to the burdens of the oppressed. Those of us who are privileged wear it like a feather; not like a feather in a cap or some showy accessory, but like a tiny feather left on our shoulder after we take off a down-filled winter coat. A feather we don't notice, we didn't put there, we don't feel. A white feather. For us even to notice its presence requires a good look in the mirror (a mere glance typically won't do it), or for someone to point it out for us. When we see it, this white feather, this privilege, we wonder who else noticed it. How long has it been there? Where did it come from? Why haven't we noticed it before?

Privilege is weightless for the privileged. Or, at least, privilege unnoticed, unnamed, or unaccepted is weightless for the privileged. Weightlessness is implicit to privilege because the weight of our privilege is being borne by those who aren't. For them, our small, white, weightless feather carries the burdens of history, oppression, exclusion, and so much more. For them, the weight of our feather is often unbearable.

So, what happens when we privileged start to understand this weight, even as we haven't previously felt it or carried it for ourselves? When someone exposes our privilege, the weightlessness of that feather begins to change. When the social and cultural systems that have upheld our privilege and distributed its weight to others begin to evolve, that feather becomes a symbol of things we never knew or understood about ourselves.

We feel embarrassed. Shamed. Confused. Indignant. Humbled. Angry. Lost. Defensive.

The shifting of power can rattle the core identity of the white male who believes he is supposed to dominate politics, the boardroom, the factory floor, or household, but no longer feels so dominant. This shifting antagonizes and undermines the singularity of one religious narrative, creating space for other beliefs, valuing dialogue over dogma. It surfaces and challenges our judgment and pity of those less fortunate, those with disabilities, those with mental illness. Suddenly, this soft, feathery lightness of privilege rips violently at the meaning and history of our whiteness, maleness, faith, socio-economic status, gender identity, mental and physical abilities. It shakes our foundation, and we don't typically like our foundation being shaken. After all, we are standing on it.

And, when this happens, we privileged choose one of two paths forward: we grow and evolve given this enlightenment, rebuilding a broader and stronger foundation, distributing power we had unjustly possessed, or we retrench and defend our pre-enlightenment state hording power and clinging to our past, now fractured, foundation. If we choose the latter, we also must understand that we are reinforcing other peoples' oppression. It isn't just about us.

The Burden of Internalized Oppression

Complicit with privilege, oppression is a constant and persistent burden. Like privilege, when unacknowledged by the oppressed, it becomes a fact of life unquestioned and unchallenged as it is unknown. Instead of manifesting in lightness, oppression is weight. As I have made clear, I fall in the privileged category. I do not know oppression first-hand in any way, shape, or form. I have merely observed it through my upbringing and my work and I have read and learned about it as a way of deepening my understanding of my own privilege.

I fought against it every day when I worked with youth. The depth and breadth of assumptions and judgments they had about their own poverty, blackness, age, and even neighborhood, our neighborhood, were stunning and troubling – even to someone who thought himself enlightened. In fact, their internalized negative assumptions were the ultimate barrier not only to achieving the dreams they still had individually (their oppression yet only partially internalized) but also to the improvement of our schools and community. Their oppression was both individual and structural, implicit in their schools and community and fueling their early process of internalization. We had to start our work with every young person by helping them think critically about what they had internalized and how that impacted the choices they made and the opportunities they sought.

Internalized oppression changes the way we dream. I recall one simple and brief conversation with a young woman who lived in public housing in a rather chaotic family situation who had told me she wanted to be a dental hygienist. I told her I thought that was great and asked her why she wanted to do that. As she talked, she expressed a broad interest in dentistry, the science, the business, the people. So, I asked without thinking why she didn't want to become a dentist rather than a dental hygienist. It left her somewhat dumbfounded, which left me dumbfounded. It had never crossed her mind. It was the first thing that crossed mine.

Our work trying to liberate each other from our oppressions (and privilege for me) was often brutal work and had to be done in a safe way and in a manner in which we had time and space to deal with anger and confusion and more questions that it spurred for them about themselves, about the adults in their lives, the systems that were supposedly there to support them. As they became more critical and more liberated, they also began to feel that burden of oppression more fully. We were externalizing it. They went from living but never seeing it to seeing it everywhere they turned, while still living it. This was powerful work, but it was dangerous work. These youth needed to see their oppression so they could begin to liberate themselves from it, reclaim power from it, but it wasn't something we could immediately just go out and change. We had to start small and individual and work from there.

While all of my youth and most of my community could point at and name experiences when they were treated differently because of their race, or their age, or their perceived income or whatever, they mostly processed those at the level of the interaction, focusing on the individual experience. They never saw the system that was supporting their marginalization; the structures that consistently and persistently delivered the same type of negative message to everyone like them. One of the stories we used to help process this growing awareness of systemic and institutional forces was the

Parable of the Boiling Frog. While simple and fairly grotesque, the Parable of the Boiling Frog illustrates the fact that a frog that is dropped into boiling water will scramble for its life to get out. This obviously makes sense to most of us and is how we would react to such pain or danger. On the other hand, if that frog is dropped into room temperature water that slowly rises to a boil, it will never even try to escape. The frog will make incremental adaptations to survive the environment that ultimately leads to its death.

This is the story of internalized oppression. We adapt to messages about our worth, about our possibility, about the quality of our character or our family or community one message at a time. And, when those messages all align in a way that consistently and persistently tells us we are lesser then we begin to believe we are lesser. At some point, we accept the fact that we are lesser. We accept our slow death without ever even recognizing it.

So, how do we get out of that slowly boiling pot? Even as personal enlightenment and liberation unfold, the systems and structures of oppression are generations in the making and will be generations in the dismantling. Just because we liberate our minds doesn't mean the systems are ready to change. We have to transform our personal liberation into something that impacts the world around us. Lest we become overwhelmed by this responsibility, we must remind ourselves that we have the chance to impact the world not just through grand social actions but through every interaction. We have the power to open hearts with every conversation, liberate minds by modeling our own liberation, by putting our own challenges and development out there for others to see, to find solace and motivation in.

Power and Powerlessness in Words

The true moment of transformation (occurs) when people have a language to describe their oppression as oppression; a following stage occurs when people envision themselves working individually and collectively to challenge oppressive conditions.[5]

– Ernest Morrell

Liberation starts with language. I started our discussion of power by focusing on the way the myriad words we use to describe it actually make understanding it more difficult, and how clarifying our language is critical to aligning people around our work. Now, I briefly want to shift our discussion of power to that of perceived powerlessness, not surprisingly with a story of the language of powerlessness.

I had lunch a dozen years later with one of the first youth I ever worked with, James, Class of 2004. He had moved back to town and we were catching up and thinking through networking, job opportunities, and that kind of thing. In moving, he had left a job where he was working with students in an alternative school, young people from the same kind of community we had worked in, but more acute, more intense. I was glad to know he had translated some of his youth experiences into doing this kind of work, but I was stunned when he told me he actually still used one of my discussion topics in his own work. I couldn't believe he still remembered it. It was one of those conversations I had facilitated almost

---

[5] Morrell, Ernest. *Critical Literacy and Urban Youth Pedagogies of Access, Dissent, and Liberation*. Florence: Taylor and Francis, 2015.: 131. Print.

certainly when I had hit peak frustration, and you never really know how those will work out.

Even back when I worked with youth, we talked about language pretty frequently. We discussed language in terms of communication, power, privilege, and how we need to keep asking "why" to blow up racial, economic, and cultural assumptions. I had a whole workshop on how "why" was the most important word in the English language. But, this time, as James reminded me, I picked four specific words. These weren't words we used as a group, or even ones that some of them had ever even heard before. I picked these four words because I felt my team needed them in their vocabularies. I picked these four words because they articulated the things we felt, experienced, and saw every day in our community and needed to name. I picked these four words because we couldn't get anywhere with our work, with exploding issues of oppression, with becoming youth advocates and organizers, with trying to change systems without understanding and attacking them.

So, what were the words that James reminded me of?

Apathy
Complacency
Lethargy
Atrophy

These aren't *the* four words, or the *best* four words. They were probably just the four words burning in my brain as I walked to work that day, stewing on how to incite and awaken our team and our community. We discussed what they meant, according to the dictionary and our localized interpretations. I asked if they had any examples. I asked them why they thought we were discussing these words. I asked them to take the next few days and to keep these words at the top of their minds, to go back home, to school, and to their neighborhood and watch for these words to surface in their experiences. I asked them to bring those observations back to the group. How do their observations relate to better strategies for our work? How do they enlighten pathways for increasing college access for students in our schools? How do they inform our efforts at keeping people away from predatory lenders?

Too often, we look at words merely as a medium for expressing our thoughts, communicating to others, written or verbal. We don't spend enough time thinking of the power of words to help us formulate our thoughts, to reflect, to liberate us, to help us name and identify and begin to understand our oppressions or opportunities. We don't think about the intellectual and creative force of words that are never written or spoken, the words churning in our minds as we seek to navigate and understand our world. These four words for me, on that day, at that time, with those young people were the most dangerous words I could think of. They were the words that could determine a future, define a community. They were the words I needed our team to own and understand, to shock our team into a more creative place, to liberate us from the words themselves.

Power as a Condition

If you doubt your power, you give power to your doubts.
– Honore de Balzac

Mastering yourself is true power.

- Lao Tzu

While I have spent a lot of time on the constructs of power, I want to shift now to the power that can actually liberate us all, the power that can upend those structures; the power that is within each of us, that is a condition of our basic humanity.

As we have discussed, privilege is a construct of power, the result of power supported by social, cultural, and economic systems. Oppression is its imposed construct of powerlessness, also the result of social, cultural, and economic systems. To understand power and to know power only as a construct, however, is to focus more on the role it plays in controlling our lives (external power) than the opportunities we have to use it to create the lives we want to live (internal power). The process of liberation is the movement of the primary locus of power from external back to internal. Granted, it is harder to find and believe in our power when we are oppressed by structures created to control and manage it, but it is still there, within us, even if latent. Fuel un-ignited is still fuel.

If there were any question about this, we can simply look again to the children of the Civil Rights Movement, who had no obvious socially, culturally, or economically constructed power, but found and organized and leveraged the implicit condition of their power to change that fact. These seemingly powerless individuals and groups knew the power of peace and love within themselves and their nonviolent community and ignited it to fight for justice for all.

For a more contemporary example, we can also look at the Arab Spring where seemingly powerless multitudes, who each individually decided they had had enough state-sponsored violence and oppression, organized revolutions that challenged, overturned, and toppled governments across the Middle East and North Africa. Most of these were also nonviolent revolutions. They too were led by young people. These peaceful revolutionaries were met with extraordinary violence deployed to protect the existing power constructs. While not all of the uprisings were successful, they triggered a global awareness of the tyranny these protestors were living under and the power of people to do something about it. After the Arab Spring, the oppressed worldwide had a contemporary model and a new hope that they may too rise up and change the systems of structural oppression in their countries.

In the United States, most of us have in the last couple of years become familiar with Black Lives Matter. Many of us know this phrase as a statement of protest and a loose movement to make its titular message a reality in our society. All of us have now seen a video of white police officers using unnecessary force on a black citizen. We've seen videos of inexplicable losses of life. We have watched rallies and even riots against and in the defense of police officers. Many of us have been left stunned and in disbelief. But, here's the thing: for black Americans, the actions of police that they are protesting have occurred for generations, really throughout the history of our country in one way or another. They aren't in disbelief or stunned. They're tired of it. And, for all this time, white people and other people of privilege have known nothing about it, or at least have paid little attention, willfully or not. There is nothing new about the realities Black Lives Matter has lifted to our country's consciousness. The organizing of Black Lives Matter and the fuel of the ubiquitous videos has surfaced the power of black lives, the power of black victims of police brutality, and the families who have been left behind. While a resolution is certainly unclear at this point, that the country, from local police to the President, is not only aware of issues with policing but actively investing in the issue illustrates the power the people have, when we organize with purpose, and put our power into action.

Whether manifest as a movement or not, power is everywhere. I challenge you to go through one day intensely aware of power in everything you see and do. I challenge you to observe power the way I asked my youth to observe complacency, lethargy, apathy, and atrophy. Focus not only on what happens but what doesn't happen in the constant exchange of power among people and institutions. In every human interaction, there is the possibility of someone making your day or perhaps ruining it, of them teaching you something, or you them. The smile. The nod. The laugh. The opening of a door. The friendly hello, or the lack thereof. Sit at the coffee shop and watch where people sit or don't sit, how they interact, how they talk to each other or don't. Stare out the window at the sidewalk and just watch. Reflect on the interactions you have in the office or wherever you work. Play back in your mind your recent interactions with your family or those closest to you. Where do you see power? What does it look like? Where do you see something more structural, oppressive, or an articulation of privilege? Just observe. Don't judge.

Remember, you are looking for power. Try to keep your mindset neutral and just note what you see. Once you stop and see power, it never goes back into hiding.

Personal and Positional Power

"Any leader's power is the product of broader social and political relations – constantly under construction, being reinforced or undermined, even as that person remains in an official leadership role. A sense of powerfulness is produced in relationships. It is rarely reliably permanent or able to be completely controlled by an individual. Such contradictory and shifting experiences of powerfulness and powerlessness can only be explained with a more sophisticated understanding of power than current leadership accounts offer." [6]

- Amanda Sinclair

"The more powerful you are, the more your actions will have an impact on people, the more responsible you are to act humbly. If you don't, your power will ruin you, and you will ruin the other." [7]

- Pope Francis

Another way to think about power-as-construct versus power-as-condition is through the lens of personal and positional power. Personal power is that power that is sourced from our individual attributes, the ways we relate to and affect others. It is built upon things like perceived expertise, likeability, perceived legitimacy, effort, and commitment. It is really about

---

[6] Sinclair, Amanda. *Leadership for the disillusioned: moving beyond myths and heroes to leading that liberates.* Crows Nest, N.S.W.: Allen & Unwin, 2007: 76. Print.
[7] https://www.ted.com/talks/pope_francis_why_the_only_future_worth_building_includes_everyone?language=en #t-949233

character traits that inspire or motivate a group to lend or defer their power – to follow. It's about personal relationships and interpersonal dynamics – even if at a distance. Positional power, on the other hand, is the power we source from formal constructs, the social, cultural, and economic apparatuses that slot us into roles. It is built on structural characteristics like access to information, visibility, and influence. It is about formal leadership titles. It's about organizational relationships and system constructs.

Despite the conceptual distinction, it is worth emphasizing that we rarely, if ever, find someone who represents an isolated instance of either personal or positional power. The two typically work hand-in-hand. At different times and in differing circumstances, an individual's personal power can be predominant while at others it's their positional. Barack Obama was a junior Senator when he first came onto the national stage at the 2004 Democratic National Convention. I, for one, knew nothing about him. I had never even heard of him. As a junior Senator, I knew he was young and probably not very influential, so his selection to speak at the Convention must have been setting him up for opportunities when he was less junior, many years down the road. In other words, relative to others in the Senate, his positional power was minimal. Then, he spoke.

In minutes, Obama's personal power, delivered through powerful words and compelling oratory had me floored. I still knew nothing about him except for those few minutes of words. His personal power had reached me through a television set. Four years later, of course, he became President. He was elected to the most powerful position in the world. The position of President, however, with the breadth of responsibilities and challenges and the constant obstruction of Congress, actually marginalized his personal power in many ways – even as he was positionally "the leader of the free world." To be clear, I don't think this is wholly unique to President Obama. I think people often run for office based on their personal power, backed up by some experience and resume of positional power, but then are left to govern from an entirely different reality. Their personal power gets inserted into an extraordinarily complex power structure that is premised on checks and balances to both personal and positional power. The genius of the Founding Fathers was creating a power structure that functioned for the purposes of governing in a Democracy while prohibiting the rise of the personally powerful, tyrannical individual leader who could destroy the Democracy. When we elect powerful individuals and send them to Washington to "do something" and they don't, the power structure is working mostly as designed.

Ironically, President Trump ran against this very safeguard and was elected by the people's frustration about the inaction of Washington. He too leveraged exceptional personal power and the positional power of both celebrity and being a billionaire businessman. Early in his Presidency, those who supported him are starting to see how structurally difficult it is to actually get things done – to "drain the swamp" as he put it. For some, this is leading to disillusionment and for other more staunch anti-Washington supporters it is just more proof of why they elected him. Those on the left, while fearing the demagoguery and anti-democratic ideals Trump has espoused, are still infuriated by his efforts, but should also find comfort in the fact that the press is still viable, walls still aren't funded, and travel bans have been revised and are still caught in the courts. Power is in check.

Unlike the checks and balances structured into our Democracy, however, our communities, our workplaces, and our relationships interlace personal and positional power in organic and often in less visible ways. Even when we don't see or recognize the power dynamics that impact our work, they are there. They are a source of both opportunity and immense challenge.

I have worked with dozens of groups over the years who were organizing around one important issue or another: gender rights, economic justice, educational opportunity, predatory lending, racial profiling, and the list could go on. These groups always come together initially with a strong sense of passion and purpose – their personal power aligns for the initial effort. As their work builds and matures over time, however, they often need more structure, and formal and informal positions develop or are explicitly created to mirror growing responsibility and the need for accountability. This generates inevitable tension in relationships. Whether we are growing and changing as a startup, a social movement, an established organization, or anything else, there is no single right answer for how we should navigate the dynamics of personal and positional power, but, navigate them, we must. We have to evaluate constantly what we are trying to accomplish, refine the strategies we should deploy, and invest in the powerful relationships that will sustain it all.

PART II:
Powerful Relationships

Nothing can stop the power of a committed and determined people to make a difference in our society. Why? Because human beings are the most dynamic link to the divine on this planet. Governments and corporations do not live. They have no power, no capacity in and of themselves. They are given life and derive all their authority from their ability to assist, benefit, and transform the lives of the people they touch. All authority emanates from the consent of the governed and the satisfaction of the customer.[8]

– John Lewis

---

[8] Lewis, John. *Across that bridge: life lessons and a vision for change.* New York: Hachette , 2016: 6. Print.

Relationships in Three Dimensions

Despite an unusual career that includes community organizing, teaching, educational consulting, nonprofit management, and co-founding a software company, I am first and foremost an artist. It has been the lessons of artmaking that have helped me process the world and push myself continuously to learn over the decades since my first studio art class. It has been the model of creating, communicating, and engaging an audience through art that has helped me create and deliver meaningful work at every step along my life's journey.

In my first sculpture class, for example, I learned that a three dimensional piece of sculpture communicates and interacts with its viewer (and the viewer with it) in all three dimensions. This seems somewhat obvious, but it's not that simple. In other words, a sculpture's depth, width, and height (along with other elements like color, texture, and movement, that live on that depth, width, and height) each communicate based on the relative size, viewing position, and experience of the viewer as he engages the sculpture. So, if an artist is trying to communicate and create a relationship with a viewer through the experience of a sculpture, he had better consider it fully in three dimensions.

While not all of us sculpt, the principles here for engaging others are relevant to every relationship, and therefore pertinent to reimagining how we conceive of power. We obviously live in at least three dimensions; so, our experiences and interactions all exist in at least three dimensions. Time can be considered a fourth. But, as we interact, process, and learn from our world, how many of us truly consider and invest in it in all three dimensions. Do we truly explore our world from all angles, or just continually process it from one vantage point, that of our own personal experience? Our frame of reference. Our power position. Do we communicate in 3D? Do we observe in 3D? Do we see and understand others in 3D?

Using this mental model from sculpture, we can apply a simple 3D frame for defining the power dynamics that inform how we relate to the world and those around us.

Dimension 1: Direct experience – my experience of a relationship, image, event, circumstance, etc. This is the "I" dimension.

Dimension 2: Divergent perspectives – others' experiences of a relationship, image, event, circumstance, etc. The "you" dimension.

Dimension 3: Determining the implications – The interactions between and implications of dimensions 1 and 2. The "we" dimension.

To truly understand my direct experience, I must be willing and able to reflect on and analyze my own perceptions and responses to various stimuli. I need to be able to identify the emotions that are, or are not, involved in my experience. I need to understand what the experience means to me, and how or why it either resonates or does not. I need to clarify the messages I receive as I understand them and see how they mesh with the messages I perceive to have been intended. Finally, I must try to identify what piece of myself I project on my perception of others' intentions. Whether it is a personal relationship, a piece of art, a work or life event, or even news or social media message, my experience is biased by who I am, how I understand the world, and even where I am at the given moment of the experience. It is rooted in my frame of reference. It is neither objective nor absolute, just as my power in relationship to others and to the triggering stimulus is neither objective nor absolute.

This is why being open to the second dimension, divergent perspectives, is so critical: it's the same complex web for the "other" experiencing the very same relationship, piece of art, work or life event, news or social media message. They bring all of their complexity to it too. It is their "I" experience. If we are to relate genuinely with others, we must understand, or at least empathize with (we still don't have to like) each other's "I" experience. We must be open to the individual bases for our respective understandings of that experience. We have to realize that there is not ever a truly common human experience; there is no fundamental truth at the level of human interaction. All perspectives and experiences are at some level divergent. In other words, the "I" experience and the "you" experience are never exactly the same. So, if we are to expand our lives to living and leading in a second dimension, we must focus not merely on our understanding the event or other triggering stimulus, but also understanding the experience of that stimulus by others.

So, let's assume for the moment that each of us is truly invested in understanding the other, committed to living in the second dimension. Now, we have to understand how our unique and divergent experiences impact the nature of our relationship, and in return, our subsequent experiences of dimensions 1 and 2. We have to determine the interactions between and implications of "I" and "you" on "we". This third dimension is the space between you and I that, while dependent on each of us, also generates its own dynamics and has its own independent characteristics. We have all had relationships whose descriptions defy the attributes of the individuals involved. Relationships develop their own "personalities." Unless we live in complete isolation, the world of "we" is the "real" world, and most of the challenges of this "we" dimension lie in our failures to deeply engage the "I" and "you" dimensions. We often fail to acknowledge that this relational dimension is a new and distinct entity – a sculpture perhaps.

While they may seem complicated, these principals can be distilled into a simple Venn diagram to help visualize the idea better. We can also use the visualization to facilitate a reflection process that functions as a great workshop to try with a team or anyone we are bringing together to accomplish something. In other words, it's a good process for anywhere we are trying to build powerful relationships.

Start by drawing three large circles on the wall like you see in Figure 1. Label the left circle "I", the middle circle "We", and the right circle "You".

Figure 1: Relationships in 3 Dimensions

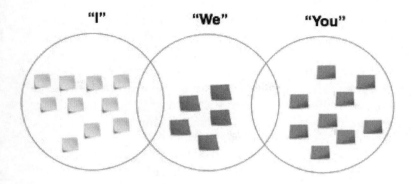

Ask your team or group to think of a time when they really worked well as a team. This could be reflecting on the previous performance of the team itself or, if it is a new team, could just be any time when they worked on a team and thought it worked well. Ask them to reflect silently for a couple of minutes about that experience. Who was there? What were they doing? What were they trying to accomplish? What was good about it? What resulted from it? Why?

Then, ask them each to think about what they as individuals did to make that team work well. What roles did they play? How did they relate to the other members? Where did they step up or step back? What did they actually do? What didn't they do? Again, this is just about them. This is to capture the "I" dimension of the effective team experience. Either using post-it notes or writing directly in the circles, capture as many attributes or descriptions of the effective "I" in team as you can.

After those are captured, prompt the group to think about what others did or didn't do to make the effective team experience. What roles did they play? How did they act? Relate to others? And, so forth. After some quiet time to think, capture as many of these attributes and descriptions of the effective "you" in team as you can.

You might want to pause here and just open the conversation for brief reflections. What do people see as common themes between the "I" and "you" circles? Are there surprises? Contradictions? Things missing that they would have expected?

Finally, we want to define the "we" experience. Again, take a few moments of individual critical reflection to consider why this particular team or team experience worked better with "I" and "you" working together. What could we accomplish together that we could not have individually? What did we learn working together that we would not have individually? How did working together make it more meaningful? More impactful? Capture these thoughts and ideas in the middle circle. Once the ideas are up, ask the group if they see any themes in the "we" circle and document those themes.

To wrap up the process, the team should discuss how and why each of the three circles must be invested in and discern the implications for time, resources, and expectations for the team and what they are trying to accomplish together. In other words, how do "I", "you" and "we" generate the power we need to accomplish our goals?

Working in the "we" domain means not only investing in ourselves and others but investing in the collective - us together. In my opening story about Special Olympics Arizona, I described an exceptional, and in many ways simple, example of this sort of commitment. Each member of the team participated with their responses to my prompt as they were able. Each listened to others'. And, when the young woman was struggling with her response, the commitment to her individual voice paid them back many times over in their understanding of their collective work.

Surfacing that voice, however, especially for the marginalized, means working through, around, and directly at systems that keep people with disabilities or any other group on the margins. In other words, our relationships have additional relationships to social, cultural, and economic systems. We can all agree that this young woman had a powerful voice and her own story to tell. We can also all agree that too many children with intellectual and physical disabilities are structurally, systematically prevented from surfacing and using their voices. This is true for all socially, culturally, or economically marginalized communities. It's manifested in anything from overt voter suppression of people of color to the fact that we casually use terms like "in the closet" to categorize LGBT friends who don't feel able, allowed, or safe to be themselves.

Powerful relationships are not just ones that impact us as participants in the relationship but are also ones that impact the world, either by their example or by direct impact. In *Creating Matters*, I introduced a creative tension model that is fundamental to putting power into action with others, for connecting purpose to power, for building powerful relationships. Not surprisingly, the basic premise of the model is that our most meaningful and powerful work happens with and through other people, in the "we" dimension.

Powerful relationships require tension, or specifically, creative tension. We all know the difference between creative and destructive tension, even if we haven't had the words to articulate their differences clearly. We have all felt them. Most of us have worked on some sort of group project, whether at work or in the studio or in the community, where we started out with a lot of energy and a lot of ideas. The initial creative tension kept ideas and pertinent topics top-of-mind, kept meetings and early brainstorming and planning high energy. We individually, and the team as a whole, felt positive and purposeful.

Most of us have also seen that kind of early creative tension quickly devolve into something less creative, less positive, and, in many cases, downright destructive. Big ideas need to be turned into concrete plans. Concrete plans need people to step up and take responsibility for putting ideas into action. Stepping up to take responsibility means increasing ownership and accountability for outcomes. Division of labor among tasks and sub-projects surfaces power dynamics and creates space for dysfunction, changes in perspective, and silos. All of these possibilities, rather probabilities, can introduce destructive tension.

I do not believe that we can prevent this sort of evolution of work any more than we can pretend that implementation of work is the same as ideation. Destructive tension is natural. The question is: can we limit its impact and translate the normal evolution of our work in such a way that we can maintain creative energy as a counter force? Can we transform destructive tension back into creative tension? To do so, we need to see the evolution of our work and our relationships through some sort of independent lens, through a mental model that feels less personal than our actual, real-time experiences of these challenges. We need to be more aware and yet more detached and objective than most of us typically are in the moment.

Building Powerful Relationships

In my discussion of power, I shared a story from my days as an organizer about the power of words. I focused on apathy, lethargy, complacency, and atrophy. So, what is the fundamental problem with these concepts as they relate to creating in our work and in our communities? Why were they so scary for my community and me? These words articulate a state absent of tension, a state of disengagement, acceptance, passivity, and deference. Acquiescence. Different from more overt forms of destructive tension, they represent the covert, destructive state of no tension.

When we look at effective and purpose-driven communities, organizations, projects, and leaders and compare them to the ones that are less so, what are the differences? Why don't these words invade their realities? How do we keep them away? How can we understand where and how we gain or lose power and purpose so that we can better lead and manage creative tension over time? How do we build relationships that are strong foundations for our work?

Let's start with a visual. Picture a rubber band; not a loop, but the kind you get when you do physical therapy, literally just a length of rubber band, maybe three feet long. Now, imagine your team members are holding one end and you are holding the other. Or, imagine your boss is holding one end and you the other. Now, imagine your employees, collaborators, or partners on a project holding either end. The rubber band represents the nature of the relationship between and among you. The actions of each affect the relationship (the band) as well as the person holding the other side. "I" is holding one side. "You" is holding the other. And, the rubber band articulates the nature of "we".

As each pulls away or comes closer, the tension in the band changes and how we hold the band and the energy it takes change. When the slack is removed, the band tightens. If we flick it or give a small tug, it moves, returns to form. It makes sound. It has energy. But, if one person pulls too hard, pulling the band taut, the band actually loses movement. It no longer changes form. The intensity of its coiled up energy generates fear and uncertainty in the other (What happens if she lets go? I'm going to get popped!). It's harder to hold on, so we focus on our grip, providing a counter force to the tension we feel from the band. We are increasingly focused on ourselves and our own position and needs. It is no longer about we. This is destructive tension via over-tension.

Now, what happens if you or I relax the tension on our end? What happens if I disinvest in the relationship and let go of the band altogether? It goes limp. It has no energy, no sound, no movement. It sags. The band is just there, inert. What does this mean for the one left holding it? What about the one who let go? It is no longer about we. This lack of shared tension results in destructive tension via under-tension.

In a creative, purposeful, powerful relationship, the energy each person contributes is dynamic and dependent upon each individual's personal goals, their shared goals, their relationship, and their trust in each other. It is constantly changing. It requires vigilance and investment. So, to remain productive, we have to constantly communicate the tension we need and listen to others as they do the same. We push and pull each other. We know when the other needs to release the tension. We communicate when we need to. We know when someone dropped his end, and accept when we drop ours. Our relationships must become more dynamic and multifaceted such that the right tension becomes both intentional and intuitive.

Imagine a creative relationship you have or have had that's focused on a goal, creating something together. Reflect on when that relationship has worked well towards that goal, or when it has faltered. Now, imagine you and your partner(s) on the opposite ends of the rubber band I described. Use this image to picture the creative energy you generated or lost in that band. How did it change over time? Why? How did you lose creative tension? Get it back?

Ultimately, we need to better understand powerful relationships and how we can leverage them to develop more of them. Part of this is understanding those relationships that are less powerful, or might even be consuming our power. What are the key differences between a relationship that generates creative tension and one that produces destructive tension? There are six key elements to consider. See Table 1.

Table 1: Creative versus Destructive Tension

	Creative	Destructive
Shared purpose	Common goal that necessitates working together to accomplish	Many small goals owned individually attempting to support collective success
Ownership of work	The collective owns the goal and understands various roles, responsibilities, skills, and relationships needed to achieve the goal.	Ownership exists at the top and trickles down as directive, or is owned at the bottom and trickles up as misalignment.
Commitment to each other	All parties commit to the process of working together as part of their responsibilities and strategy in the work.	All parties focus only on doing their job rather than engaging the work of the whole.
Teaching & Learning	Everyone is a teacher and a learner.	There are teachers and there are learners.
Collective action	The act of working together creates tension that informs the purpose and nature of the work in a generative way.	Individual actions taken based on responsibilities such that there is no generative tension created as part of action, but only the tension created by results.
Group and individual reflection	The collective remains vigilant and reflective, as individuals and as a group, so that the tension remains timely and creative.	Reflection does not happen among all parties. If it happens, it is at the individual level and does not inform or evolve the structure of the work.

Shared Purpose

A truly shared purpose is an extraordinary thing. And, too often, we assume shared purpose with others because of the nature of the organization we work in, our proximity, our socio-economic similarities, or perhaps even the community we live in. But, shared purpose can never be taken for granted. It must be overt. It must be ever-present. Shared purpose is extremely hard to develop, much less maintain. Like the creative tension that generates it, shared purpose requires vigilance to keep adapting it over time while reinventing and continuously communicating and reflecting on its current form.

Sports teams are probably our culture's most obvious example of this concept. We have all seen the teams that are loaded with talent, whether in little league or the NFL, that just don't seem to win. They do well, but they get surprised or "upset" year after year by some other team not many people were paying attention to. Despite the old saying that there is no "I" in team, there is an "I" in "we" and in every relationship. The problem is when the "I" becomes too much the focus and the work and the collective suffer as a result.

The challenges of truly shared purpose were consistently an issue in my work as a consultant. In many ways, when an organization brings in a consultant – at least for the type of work I was doing - we can guess that they either don't have a sense of shared purpose across parts of the organization or perhaps that they have a sense of purpose that they do not know yet how to enact. The former results in consulting focused on internal organizational work, planning, communication and so forth. The latter is often about innovation or new products or programming, which often, in turn, illuminates the need for internal organizational work, planning and communication efforts.

I worked for several years with a national advocacy organization that wanted to deepen the role of young people in their dropout prevention efforts. They, in effect, had a new initiative around what they called "youth voice" in their campaigns, and they brought me in to do some of the direct work initially, but ultimately to help them figure out how to do it themselves. The charge seemed clear. The work was in my wheelhouse. The organization was excited to have me working with them. So, I worked for a year or so starting with the people closest to the programming and the campaigns. We worked on mindsets and tools and expectations and all things strategic and tactical around youth voice. In time, that work began to mature and youth voice was pushing the larger organization, not just the program people, to think differently about their work.

To make a long story short, the work mostly got shut down. Where we had worked on authentic youth voice, the broader organization ended up mostly just wanting to check the box. Where we were developing tools for effective relationships, the organization was just as happy with a youth survey. It was an extraordinarily demeaning and marginalizing experience for the staff and me that boiled down to inaccurate assumptions about our shared purpose around the work of youth voice.

Since this experience, I almost obsess about shared purpose with any new client. I confirm, reiterate, reflect on, and adapt our shared purpose as a fundamental part of the work, of delivering the impact the client wants and I can meaningfully deliver. I use these conversations to help maintain creative tension in my relationship with the organization and with relationships I am part of within the organization. I learned the hard way how foundational and potentially fragile shared purpose can be and how not paying attention to it can undermine years of work in no time at all.

Ownership of the Work

Ownership boils down to how we as individuals in the work carry a sense of shared purpose as part of who we are and what we are about. Too many people want to own the outcomes, but aren't willing to own the work. Or, they want to own only the positive outcomes and won't accept ownership when things don't go as expected. Perhaps they just want to own "their" work but not the work of the group as a whole. So, where does our sense of shared purpose live for us? How is it manifest in the work we are doing together? How does it persist when I am working alone? If we own our work deeply, we will carry it with us wherever we go. We will celebrate the victories, learn from our defeats, but more importantly, will feel the stresses and challenges of the process at a deeply personal and interpersonal level. Such depth of ownership is fundamental to sustaining motivation when times inevitably get difficult.

As a startup technology company, it was critical for our small team to all feel a strong sense of ownership in the product. In the hustle of the every day, we had to know and trust that each of us would do whatever it would take to make it work, to make the clients happy, to make the technology scalable, to make the business successful. We also had to have enough ownership to step up for each other when others needed to step back to take care of themselves. Ownership isn't just about doing more or having more accountability for tasks, it's about the whole and your being part of it. Ownership, therefore, should never be confused with the concept of buy-in. Buy-in is circumstantial and peripheral in that ownership still belongs to someone else. We buy in to their ownership, so there is little-to-no loss when we don't meet expectations. We can't build strong teams on buy-in.

Not surprisingly, we can't develop ownership of our collective work if our vision and purpose aren't aligned across the group. When developing software, I learned quickly that there are potentially at least three versions of a feature being "done." The first is that the developer has finished the code. So, he says it's done. The second is that a lead developer deploys the code. So, he says it's done. The third is that the feature actually works for the end user, which is when a product manager says it's done. I quickly realized that a major part of my job was aligning my team of developers around the idea that the end user's ability to use a feature was the ultimate definition of done that we should all be seeking - not the various technical definitions. After a few bumps and bruises and mishaps within the team, this level of end-to-end ownership of the product was what ultimately made our team and our product successful. It also allowed us to communicate and set expectations more clearly among ourselves as well as with clients. Each of us could own the parts of the work we were responsible for, but we fundamentally had to agree on what done meant. We all had to own the user experience of the end product. We had to own our collective work in delivering a quality product.

We all naturally own the work that is closest to us, a part of our experience and expectations on a daily basis –

whether that's federal policymaking, product management, fundraising, or engaging young people. We also, however, have to own the broader context of our work. Balancing ownership of the individual contribution and ownership of the broader vision is critical to maintaining creative tension among any team.

Commitment to Each Other

In many ways, commitment to each other is the operational component of a personal sense of ownership – putting ownership into practice with and through others. Commitment gets tested when things are rough, when people are stressed and work still has to get done. Who's got our back? Who's willing to do what it takes? Who sees and is invested in my personal success as fundamental to overall success? This can be in a sports team facing a comeback, an organizational team hustling to meet a deadline, a family at a critical time, or a startup just being a startup. To turn some part of our stress into creative energy, we must have a commitment to each other that outlasts the realities of our various trying circumstances.

Commitment to each other, like many ideals, is most obvious when it breaks down. When I was in business school, the students were organized in teams for the two years. For the first several months, the work was mostly individual and the team was there to help each other out, to share in each other's experiences and knowledge bases. This is how I survived Statistics as well as Accounting. During this time, however, each individual turned in his own assignment and got his own grade and so forth. For several months, our team got along great.

Then, most of the work for the rest of the two years changed into genuine group work and the "shit hit the fan" as they say. Those initial months had clearly built some commitments among sets of people within the team, but not among the team as a whole. I'll spare the gory details, but people couldn't and wouldn't make meetings; people didn't collaborate or communicate. There was no shared commitment to each other's learning and success as part of the team's. So, in fact, there was no team.

It was eye opening to see how the workload and the pressure and the self-interest obscured for some students one of the critical learning opportunities of the program – working in a team of powerful peers, navigating creative and destructive tension as the work evolved. Some of us saw that value and purpose as part of our work. Others owned their own work as the end game and ultimately lost out on the whole experience of learning how to develop powerful relationships under such intense circumstances.

Teaching and Learning

Teaching and learning are part of any creative relationship. We all must realize that we have something important to share with the world, with each other, and, if we believe that, then others do too. One of my biggest challenges in my direct community work with youth was convincing them that I didn't have all the answers – or rather, that I knew I didn't have all the answers. It wasn't so much that they thought I did but that they had spent too much time with adults who thought they did. It took months of me asking questions, intentionally making mistakes in front of them and vocally and openly accepting when I was wrong, thanking them when they taught me something, that I finally established this level of trust and creative tension.

One of the examples I have given over the years just to prove my discipline in breaking down this cultural power dynamic of adult-as-teacher and youth-as-learner was in my refusal to ever give them an answer for something they could find out for themselves. I wouldn't even provide the definition of a word if they asked. I responded with: where could you find that? That's why we ended up spending a year and a half with them researching for themselves the issues in and around college access – information they wanted to know, and could find and articulate for themselves. That's why they wrote their own white paper on the issue. I could have knocked it all out on my own in two weeks. But the process, the learning, the relationships, the commitment building that went into them doing it for themselves was the goal. The process. It wasn't about information. It was about developing advocates and strengthening their shared purpose. Once we shifted those ageist cultural dynamics, once we had some creative tension, we could work better as partners. We could have a more creative relationship as youth and adults.

In my time in software development, the teaching/learning dynamic has been uniquely complicated. I don't know how to write code. I am a product person not a programmer. So, what that effectively means is that I don't build or develop anything at all. I am at the complete mercy of a handful of really smart and talented people who stare at a screen writing and reading a language that I don't understand and that I just hope turns into the feature or functionality that I requested. It may, or may not. I really have no power other than what I have cultivated relationally in partnership with my programmers.

One of the best ways to build this relationship is through explicit teaching and learning, which requires a commitment to communication. I need my team to explain to me in non-technical terms what they are doing and why to ensure it stays aligned with the product or feature direction that I've laid out and communicated to people outside of our team. They do not need to teach me to be a programmer, but it is extremely helpful if they expose a bit of the process and logic they use in doing their work. That logic I can learn. In turn, it is incumbent upon me to explain the context and the logic of what I may request or prioritize in terms of product direction. I have to take the time to share what feedback we may be getting from the market, what business pressures we are experiencing, and why this new feature is a priority when it seems ridiculous to them. Without some level of teaching and learning, our worlds are so different that our product and our clients are the most likely to become the victims of failed teaching and learning.

Teaching and learning can and should be a part of our daily lives and interactions. I try every day, for example, to ask my kids to tell me something they learned at school that day. I want to always focus them on the learning process and I want to see what engaged them and give them the time and space to tell me about it. But, I realized recently, that I wasn't going far enough when a family friend, responding to one of my blogs, wrote that she has a friend who asks a better version of the same question: "what did you learn today that you can teach me?" This is profoundly more powerful than my prompt and has now become my question of my daughters.

Collective Action

When we started the Tennessee College Access and Success Network, our goal was to increase the number of Tennesseans with a postsecondary degree. Our team collectively knew and had already worked with a number of college access professionals and programs around the state. We started the network by building on those relationships. But, for the network not to merely be a nominal sum of its parts, for it to be more than an organization that provided an annual conference and little else, we had to determine what we collectively valued and needed to work on. How were we all stronger and our work better for being a part of the network? Answering this was not only critical to our value proposition but was also necessary to get already over-worked and under-paid, but extraordinarily passionate, college access leaders to engage in something more than their local work. Something had to inspire them to want to share their work and learn from others. Something had to motivate them to make their work bigger than their local efforts. We had to articulate a clear and collective call to action. Without this, our request would feel dubious or alternately compulsory – both of which are more likely to generate destructive rather than creative tension.

We framed our network around practices, partnerships, and policies and focused our membership recruiting efforts on getting feedback and priorities "from the field" on those topics. The early stages of our collective action were really focused on sharing learning and networking among members who did similar work. This seemingly simple orientation built enough of an action focus, a message that we weren't all talk, to rapidly build a 150-member network. Our collective action evolved to more than learning over time, as we focused on building stronger partnerships and affecting policy, but it was the overt principle and first small steps of collective action that got the network off the ground. It allowed all of our members the space and opportunity to be a part of something bigger than their local work while also enabling them to share and learn and create with others based on that local work.

Group and Individual Reflection

It is very difficult to learn the most important lessons of our lives and our work without stepping back to reflect. In the moment, we are too busy. Our emotions are too high. We are not objective. We are still experiencing it. So, reflection must be intentional and have its own space and time to be meaningful. The process itself can be individual or group, formal or informal. All are valuable and in most cases all are needed at particular times.

I have done all kinds of reflections with all kinds of people and around all kinds of work. This has been a true blessing of my career. Perhaps the most fun and productive reflections I have ever experienced, however, were in the back of a taxi in Port of Spain, Trinidad. For nine days, my colleague Terry and I were there to facilitate trainings with the Ministry of Education and the Ministry of Local Government. To get to the training location from where we were staying was a daily 45-minute drive. Terry and I had spec'd out the full nine days worth of an agenda before getting there, as one would expect. After the first day, however, we mostly threw that agenda out. On our way home after that first day, we reflected on the cultural differences and expectations and norms that were in the room, ones different than we had experienced with an American audience for example. We made some significant adjustments to how we invited audience participation and we went back the next day more prepared to meet and challenge their learning needs and expectations. At the end of that day, we got into our cab again and spent the next 45 minutes reflecting on what the participants had shared with us in their group discussions about the challenges and opportunities they faced. So, again, in the back of the cab, we retooled the entire next day's facilitation plan and protocols. We went to the hotel, slept on it, and then got back in that cab for 45 minutes the next morning to tweak and sometimes to again totally throw out our ideas for better ones we had come up with alone. And so, the nine days progressed with our work getting smarter and Terry and me getting better at delivering and reflecting on it. It was one of the most creative and deliberate, and yet completely unplanned, processes of reflection I have ever experienced and resulted in some of the best work of my career.

Here are a few simple questions that we used in the taxi and with the participants in the workshops, and have used countless time since:

1. What did you learn from the experience?
2. What surprised you about the experience? (Bonus question: why?)

3. What still feels unresolved, or, what questions do you still have?

Powerful relationships must focus on generating and maintaining the right creative tension, building environments and interactions in which tension among partners, friends, colleagues, and coworkers generates power rather than consuming it. Our work manifests from the nature of our relationships. Everything stems from them, flows through them, and depends upon them.

Sustaining Powerful Relationships

If building powerful relationships depends upon generating the right level of creative tension then sustaining them requires that we consider and evaluate our impact and our effectiveness toward what we are trying to accomplish, the thing that brought us together in the first place. In other words, powerful relationships exist within the context of powerful work. The previous section focused on the why and how of the relationship. This section focuses on the interactions our relationships have with our work and how our work can, in turn, impact those relationships – the reciprocity between work and relationships. I will focus on how the "I", "you", and "we" domains maintain purpose and create impact given the realities of actual work.

After all, relationships are relatively easy if we aren't experiencing failure, hitting roadblocks, getting feedback on our performance, and so forth. Any relationship with purpose is going to face obstacles and require resilience. As purpose grows, relationships can get a lot more complicated, but they can also get a lot more powerful, and more fulfilling, with deeper and broader purpose.

Powerful relationships are built on a sense of purpose, so we can't avoid the inevitable realities of increasing responsibility and accountability for the work we are trying to do together. In powerful relationships, we work together for a reason that is bigger than us and is bigger than our relationships – bigger than "I", "you", or "we". It is about "we" for what. "We" is a strategy for building and sustaining powerful work.

The creative tension that often drives the early stages of a powerful relationship can quickly get undermined by the weight and reality of what we hope to accomplish. The passion of a budding movement can get consumed by the work of sustaining a Movement. The excitement of an early startup can quickly dwindle as the realities of the market or of cash flow start to close the door of opportunity. Any small victory in our work often exposes a cruel reality that the next victory may be bigger, but it remains much farther away and harder to get to.

Like relationships, powerful work requires daily vigilance and commitment over time, not just in spurts. It depends on the cultivation of trust and relies on strong communication. It is premised on consistency and the steadfastness of unconditional love for each other and those we are trying to impact. Powerful work is maintained over time by an emphasis on logic and dedication to clarity of purpose and message. See Figure 2.

There are three pillars of powerful work: relationships, responsibility, and accountability. Instead of focusing on these pillars as end points, however, I focus on the relational elements that tie them together. I have emphasized the relational variables that not only link the pillars but fuel the relationships that will drive commitment and success in those pillars. Just like our visualization of creative tension with the rubber band, we can consider the space between relationships and responsibility, for example, as being characterized by the state of communication and trust between them. Similarly, the connection between relationships and accountability will be defined by consistency and unconditional love; and between accountability and responsibility by logic and clarity.

Figure 2: Sustaining Powerful Relationships

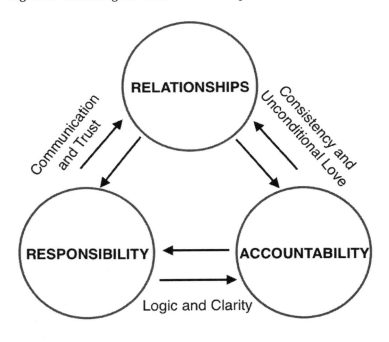

Connecting Relationships and Responsibility: Communication and Trust

Relationships and responsibility are connected by effective communication and trust. It is pretty obvious for most of us that a relationship without trust is usually a poor relationship. But, have we thought about how the quality of communication of our expectations, for example, impacts others' sense of responsibility to us and to themselves? Have we communicated to those most important to us and the work how valuable and important they are? What role they play in our lives, our work, and in living our values? Have we expressed how much we believe in them? How much we appreciate them? Do our own actions model the responsibility we seek from them, so that they can trust us? Have we given them the chance to express what they expect from us?

Responsibility, like communication, is not a one-way experience. It is an exchange, the nature of which is defined fundamentally by the level of trust among potentially responsible parties. This exchange, however, is colored by a range of factors like context, timing, medium, and perception, and is thus ever changing. We've all had relationships with ups and downs that in many ways were driven by what was happening around us. Many people have strong loving relationships with partners or friends that just come at ideal times in their lives or perhaps even the wrong times. Context and timing impact the relationship. We've all had someone say something to us at a time that we were not able to hear or receive it, provide feedback or insights on our work or behavior when we weren't ready for it. Perhaps their message was obscured by how they delivered it. Perhaps we didn't trust that they had our best interests in mind. Perhaps we just had had a bad day. This is why relationships are complex. This is why communication is complex and fundamental to trusting relationships.

Communication in all of its forms is the medium of our relationships. It is essential to who we are, how we connect to each other, and how we impact the world around us.

The Language of Communication

When my younger daughter was one, she talked constantly. Truly. Constantly. She had her own language like many young children do.

She would go on and on, high and low, back-of-the-throat to the top-of-the-lungs, making all kinds of odd and funny sounds. Her brows furrowed. Her eyes looked around for some acknowledgment. She paused. Smiled. My wife and I talked back, acknowledging, reinforcing, and doing all we could to encourage her expression. But, she quickly became frustrated.

First the arms would go up! Then they would start waving around. The hands slammed down. She arched her back, torqued her body left and right. The "sweet" sounds of a baby would be replaced by shrieking sounds of frustration. The pitch would get higher. The crying began. She was just angry. We scrambled to give her food. Water. A bottle. A toy. We picked her up. Passed her around. Tried playing peek-a-boo. Sometimes, one of these would be the right response, mostly not.

We scrambled, but failed to communicate; and it wore all of us out.

I can't help but think about how this dissonant dance of ineffective communication remains almost humorously consistent from toddler to local nonprofit to Fortune 500 (although the resulting behaviors may be slightly different). We have all worked with individuals and some of us in entire organizations that are frustrated, exasperated, and exhausted because of bad communication. We all know various versions of the give-and-take of the parent and child described in my house. We all know this process often isn't pretty between adults either. Organizational dysfunction plays out in much more dangerous ways than some smashed peas on the floor. When adults can't communicate and don't trust each other, children fall through the educational cracks; patients don't get the care they need; injustice goes unaddressed.

For the child, learning to talk isn't just about making sounds. Ultimately, the child has to learn words (or some other form of language if they have disabilities). They have to learn to string words together to make phrases and then structure sentences that others understand. They have to learn and understand context (a time and a place for certain words and topics). They learn tone. They develop their own voices and understand how this can support, or get in the way of, actually communicating. As they grow and learn, children will explore a variety of mediums to deliver their thoughts and insights and ideas, and figure out which ones work best for her and for particular audiences.

If it is this complicated for a single child, then for organizations and communities it is exponentially more so. Despite what most of us call communication in our work, it is not as simple as clicking "send". Communication is about structure, context, tone, voice, medium, and audience – just like it is for the child. And, given the complexity of organizations and the unique relationships within them, not to mention the various degrees of skill development by the people who make them up, communication requires much broader and more deliberate attention and investment than most of us are willing to admit.

The familiar refrain of "know your audience", for example, is deceptively complicated when we apply it across any large number of human beings, whether in an organization or not. Good communicators understand that they have many audiences who communicate in many different "languages" even within a single community, organization, or any collection of people for that matter. They know that these audiences like the individuals who make them up change over time. And, the right context or tone or voice or medium will vary for them at different times, literally from day to day or even hour to hour. Communication, therefore, is not a singular concept, and it is certainly not static. It isn't just something you do, or that just happens. It is a relational skill that develops, evolves, and must be actively nurtured, invested in, and evaluated. It is a skill that is premised in the philosophy that trusting relationships are the most crucial part of our work.

More than a skill then, communication is also a relational dynamic, one medium of the transfer of power between people. Contrary to most of our practices, communication doesn't start with us. It starts with our audience; and to share our power and grow theirs, we have to know their language. We have to understand their point of view, and use that to tailor our communication.

Communication That Builds Trust

Before we ask something of someone else, before we offer critique or offer insight on their work, before we press send, we should try to understand and be clear for ourselves why we are doing it. As the generators of communication, when we accept and own this responsibility then we demonstrate respect for our recipient that helps build trust over time. When we spew things out randomly, when our timing is terrible, when we leave it to the recipient of the communication to figure out what to do with it or even what it really means, to discern if it's even really for them, then we create a huge amount unnecessary angst and confusion and noise – destructive tension. We are implicitly saying that we don't respect the recipient enough to consider our words, our timing, our purpose, or why we have chosen them as the audience for the message. As a result, we are giving them a reason not to trust our communications or us.

When we think about communication that is not face-to-face, most of it these days it seems, our challenges to doing it well are magnified. We've all sent an email or text or posted something to social media with an intended tone of sarcasm or humor, for example, that simply didn't translate to the medium. We don't see our audiences, so they aren't really real to us. We email things to everyone just to make sure the people who may need to get the message get it. We all willingly spam everyone else. The problem is that if we spam people today, they're not going to trust what we send tomorrow. Ironically then, most of us are guilty of communicating exactly how we hate being communicated with. As this pattern grows exponentially in organizations or as our work speeds up and grows more intense, our message gets muddled and trust gets diminished. Our people are more distracted. Our ability to focus them on our particular message in the midst of all of the rest becomes a race to claim criticality and urgency. But, in time, when everything is critical or urgent, nothing is.

Research from the National Center for Biotechnology Information demonstrates the frightening, if humorous, effects of this reality. It also shows us that the problem is only getting worse, that our attention spans are on the decline, our communication more challenging, and our trust more tenuous. According to Table 2, our attention spans can't decline much. We are nearing zero.

Table 2: Attention Span Research

Subject and Year	Attention Span
Avg American in 2000	12 seconds
Avg American in 2015	8.25 seconds
Goldfish in 2013	9 seconds
Source: National Center for Biotechnology Information	

So, yes, officially, we Americans have a shorter attention span than a goldfish. Is it any wonder so many of us feel so mistrustful and disconnected from the religious, economic, political, and social institutions that once helped us organize our lives. At some point, this has to stop. If we are going to live and lead effectively and purposefully, we must step back from our bad habits and communicate with purpose. We need to create environments and expectations that allow others to slow down and do the same. We must help people recognize and experience our communication as an interpersonal exchange, an extension of a positive, productive relationship. We have to move from transactional communication to transformative communication.

When we are communicating with purpose, there are four main goals we are trying to accomplish with our people:

1. We want them to *know* something. We have information that we believe they want or need or will at least find valuable; or, otherwise believe they should want, need, or find valuable. We want them to know it.

2. We want them to *do* something. There is a call-to-action of some sort, or at least an expected, identifiable response, which differentiates this communication from just knowing something.

3. We want them to *feel* something. In examples from religious inspiration to bullying, getting people to feel things through communication is a powerful reflection on a relationship. We typically want people to feel something so that they decide on their own what they want to do, including doing nothing and perhaps just appreciating the feeling.

4. We want people to *engage*. We want them to feel and act and know based on their own motivations and expectations. We fundamentally want our communication to represent the positive sharing of power with others, such that we don't always have to ask them to do, and they don't always depend on us to know. See Figure 3.

Figure 3: Communicating with Purpose

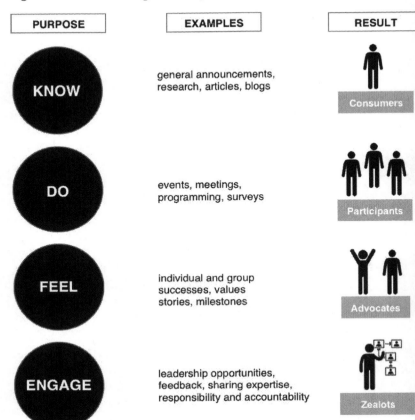

If we are honest with ourselves, we can probably agree that *know* and *do* communications far outnumber the *feel* and *engage* communications in our daily work and lives. Whether we are a neighborhood group or a major company, we focus so heavily on the day-to-day transactions of our work together that we can easily lose our purpose – a phenomenon most acute in the hectic, busy, high intensity times when we most need to be grounded in our shared values and goals. Transactional communication will deliver transactional relationships. If we want something more, we need to communicate accordingly. By knowing why we are communicating, how we hope to engage or transform our audience by sharing power with them, and aligning our communication strategy with the intended outcome, we can begin to communicate with purpose.

Connecting Relationships and Accountability: Consistency and Unconditional Love

Commitment and accountability cannot be sold. They have to be evoked.

- Peter Block[9]

Power is of two kinds. One is obtained by the fear of punishment and the other by acts of love. Power based on love is a thousand times more effective and permanent then the one derived from fear of punishment.

- Mahatma Gandhi

Without meaningful, purposeful communication, we cannot build trust. Without trust, we cannot build healthy relationships. And, without healthy relationships, accountability can feel oppositional and even oppressive. In such an absence, we are often left trying to sell or enforce accountability because we haven't established

---

[9] Block, Peter. *The answer to how is yes: acting on what matters.* San Francisco, CA: Berrett-Koehler Publishers, 2003: 178. Print.

the environments in which it can be evoked. We are left to wield our power through fear because we have failed to love.

Accountability and relationships are connected by consistency and unconditional love. Accountability must be consistently and equitably applied. If and when we screw up, we should be able to count on those who love us to hold us accountable. We also must know that we can be forgiven and that the love of those around us is unconditional. If we believe that love is conditional, then we can be irresponsible all we want and figure "well, I would have lost it at some point anyway." If I know love will always be there, I have to make choices knowing I cannot break away from it or set it aside. If love is unconditional then I am unconditionally responsible to/for it.

Love may seem a natural thing to consider when we talk about our personal relationships, but it probably seems odd to talk about it in the context of the organizations we work in. If we work from the premise that relationships are foundational to our work, however, suddenly love no longer feels misplaced, but rather required. Unconditional love means I can trust you, no matter what, no matter where we work, what we are working on, or whether we agree or disagree. It means you want what's good for me, and I for you. Leading with love means we know when to step back from what we are doing, and check in on how we are being. Love is celebrating others' successes and helping them safely process and learn from their failures. Love is communicating thoughtfully and with empathy. Love is listening. Love is consistency. As Paulo Freire writes: *"Dialogue cannot exist...in the absence of a profound love for the world and for people...Love is at the same time the foundation of dialogue and dialogue itself...Because love is an act of courage, not of fear, love is commitment to others."* [10]

If we believe this, then love is clearly at the center of all of our work with others. It must be unconditional or we revert to instability, uncertainty, and a lack of trust in our relationships. We have to work at love. We have to develop the tools to manage ourselves and our emotions and daily challenges such that they do not disrupt the roots of love but rather return us to those roots for nourishment when times are difficult. Love has to be more than something we show. It must be *of* our actions, intrinsic to how we treat and engage with others.

Love requires, therefore, deliberate effort, and consistency as an act of love requires commitment and skill. Consistency, like power itself, is a relational dynamic. It's not enough to believe my own actions and messages are consistent if others who receive or observe them experience them otherwise. This is why group reflection is so critical; to surface these perceptions and to promote continuous improvement.

In today's environment of social media and overexposure, however, the concept of consistency has become exceedingly complicated. With so little left private, consistency becomes a necessary part of every interaction, not just those in a given context. It no longer suffices to be a consistently ethical leader in our organizations, but prove to be otherwise in our community, or vice versa. In the age of transparency and access to information, consistency is the offspring of integrity as C.S. Lewis described it: "Integrity is doing the right thing, even when no one is watching." Now, more than ever, even if no one is watching or we think

---

[10] Freire, Paulo. *Pedagogy of the oppressed.* New York: Continuum, 2000: 89. Print.

no one is listening, they probably are. At a minimum, the likelihood is higher than ever that either our praiseworthy or ignominious actions will surface and echo eventually through our networks and then the networks of those networks.

Unlike the simplistic consistency of media ideologues or the entrenched, partisan politicians who dominate the morning shows with "consistent" messages, consistency as part of powerful relationships should not be confused with staking out a position and sticking with it no matter what. It is not about redundancy. It is as much about process as message. Consistency in powerful relationships is about patterns of behavior and decision-making across many, and ideally all, contexts that instill trust in others. Contrary to many of our beliefs, consistency can and should be malleable and adaptable. Consistency should involve learning and growing. Consistency requires transparency. Consistency, as perceived by others then, is also a matter of expectations.

Obviously consistency as being predictably mean, divisive, or abusive is not part of powerful relationships, but rather an example of someone trying to be a powerful individual by consistently claiming power from others in a relationship. If I expect you to verbally abuse me, for example, and you do, then clearly this doesn't build our relationship or my sense of responsibility to you. At best, it may spur some accountability motivated by an attempt to avoid that behavior or experience again, but this is fleeting. As obvious as this distinction might sound, we should recognize how pervasive mean, divisive, and abusive behavior is in our relationships and our cultural concept of power. Look no further than our national partisan politics.

This isn't just a part of politics, however. I once had the superintendent of a large urban school district tell me "I rule by fear because fear works." Well, it doesn't. And, it didn't. Early promise of improvement in his tenure were undermined by disastrously low morale at all levels, flight of talent, and a culture of backstabbing and ass-covering that had nothing to do with educating children. Fear was initially interpreted as a sort of consistent command-and-control structure until the structure collapsed. He and his people were effectively run out of town. Temporary affect should not be mistaken for powerful leadership; submission should not be confused for followership.

Consistency as a complement to unconditional love allows us to develop a sense of responsibility and connection with our people. It paves the pathway between responsibility and accountability. Only through a sense of personal responsibility will we each truly accept our own accountability. And, with a deep sense of responsibility to others, my accountability to you is wrapped up in my accountability to myself.

Urgency and Grace

Consistency and unconditional love, more than any other part of sustaining powerful relationships, require a sense of grace, for ourselves and others. We are never as consistent as we think we are, or try to be. It's also really difficult for most of us to love people we can't stand, those whose values stand in direct opposition to our own. Love for most of us is bound to a concept of affection or a feeling rather than a fundamental value of our way of being, but the depth of the unconditional is more philosophy than affectation or emotion. If communication and building trust are key strategies for powerful relationships, consistency and unconditional love are the core values. Like anything aspirational, even spiritual, we will fall short of their calling often, perhaps more times than not, and sometimes in very visible ways.

Grace is about doing this well, about understanding our basic, common humanity, and accepting our human limitations, in ourselves and others. Urgency is about our aspiration to be and do more despite our limitations. Grace is about forgiving ourselves. Urgency is about never accepting excuses. Grace is about loving ourselves and others unconditionally. Urgency is about challenging ourselves relentlessly. Grace without urgency gets little accomplished. Urgency without grace delivers certain burnout. Urgency and grace represent the ebb and flow of living with purpose while ensuring we, our relationships, and our work are built to last.

If we don't have grace, then our failings will invite us to lower our aspirations, which not only diminishes something of ourselves, but also of our relationships and our work. We must be bigger than our failures. We must accept them as part of working with purpose. If we aren't working with a sense of urgency, on the other hand, we have to question how deeply we own our sense of purpose. If we aren't learning and growing rapidly, searching for answers relentlessly, wanting to be better, then we probably aren't really using our power in ways that matter that much to us.

In my role as a parent, I am more aware of the balance of urgency and grace than I've ever been. I see the parenting of my two daughters as the ultimate testing ground, the endurance test, the crucible for powerful relationships. Every day, my relationship with my daughters evolves, and therefore, to some degree my relationship with my wife. Every day my sense of purpose as a parent is the most present, the most urgent thing in my life. Every day my girls learn something new and present me with a surprise, a new question, a novel perspective, or a new word or phrase that I get to help them understand and define. They change so rapidly and their personalities are unfolding with such force that consistency is as much a philosophy and creative enterprise as it is a commitment to a core set of rules and expectations. I am destined to fail and to do so frequently. If I am all urgency and no grace with myself as a parent, then the stress of my daily failures will overwhelm my ability to reflect and improve.

After all, sometimes I'm just tired. Sometimes my kids are just frustrating. Sometimes I don't know what to do and sometimes I do the wrong thing just because it's the easiest in the moment. As a result, sometimes I sit them down and say I'm sorry, that I love them no matter what, that I don't have all the answers, that I am doing the best I can. I want them to know this. I don't want them to experience some moment of disillusionment down the road when they unexpectedly realize I am just as human as they are. They can know that now. They can begin developing empathy now. I'd rather be as open and honest as is appropriate, so if nothing else, they will learn to be open and honest, to be humbly flawed and resilient human beings along with me.

I share my perspective on parenting here because I want you to consider that last paragraph and replace the context of my children with neighbors, coworkers, employees, or most any other human being you interact with. The aspiration for transparency and humility remain valid even if it feels foreign to the realities of some of those relationships as they exist today. This comparison is not in any way to suggest some angle of paternalism in our relationships. In fact, it's the opposite. It's about moving the power from me to others, so that we are collectively more powerful. Every day, I try to bring some basic humanness to my actual paternalism (parenting), as well as to my formal and informal work with others. I believe that deep humanness is part of any powerful relationship.

It's important to note that this power in humanness includes allowing others, including my children, to fail; to fail with grace and learn and recover with a sense of urgency. What better way to show people they have power and that we love them unconditionally than to instill a sense of ownership in them and their work and their choices, especially when they aren't successful? It is easy to own success, but far more challenging to learn to own failure. We demonstrate our consistency and unconditional love not by preventing their failure but by always being there to show a little grace, helping them process, learn, and grow when it happens.

Connecting Responsibility and Accountability: Logic and Clarity

Accountability is something that is left when responsibility has been subtracted.

- Pasi Sahlberg

In 2013, Microsoft acquired the failing Nokia mobile phone business in a deal that Nokia leadership had clearly hoped to avoid. In media reports at the time, the

Nokia CEO, visibly saddened, lamented: "we didn't do anything wrong, but somehow, we lost." I feel for the guy and for any of the employees who were negatively impacted by Nokia's mobile phone business collapse. But, how can the CEO of a company make such a statement? Yes, the market changed. Yes, technology changed. Yes, things got a lot more competitive. And, his job as the leader of the company was to help the company adapt to all of this and continue to thrive despite it. Rapid change, competition for resources, and leading change are the same realities facing a community organizer or the head of a nonprofit organization or any other group. Clearly, adapting to rapid change is much easier said than done, and there are going to be times when change happens so fast that we may not actually be able to adapt and thrive. However, that's not really the point. Nokia didn't adapt fast enough under his leadership which led to their shedding their mobile phone business; but still he claimed they did nothing wrong.

The only way a CEO of a company that was once the industry leader but ended up failing can claim it did nothing wrong is if there is some standard by which he holds himself accountable that doesn't relate to the overall health and survival of the business. He must have believed in some way that his ultimate responsibility as the CEO was not in perpetuating the success of the company. He must have had some different logic or a lack of clarity as to what he was responsible and accountable for. Otherwise, he simply couldn't make this statement. Holding ourselves accountable merely for doing nothing wrong and taking responsibility when everything goes wrong are philosophically in opposition. The CEO's comments illustrate how responsibility and accountability can lose connection with each other and what can happen when they do.

Powerful relationships require that responsibility and accountability stay connected, two sides of the same dynamic, purposeful coin. Logic and clarity are the facilitators of this connection. If I don't understand the logic of what I am being held accountable for, I am not likely to feel responsible for it, even if I feel responsible to a relationship. If I understand my accountability, but I really don't buy the logic behind it - and also perhaps have not bought in to the relationship that supports it - I am not likely to feel truly responsible for it. Both of these define the path to Pasi Sahlberg's version of accountability as a sort of residue left behind when responsibility is gone. We must ensure that our people understand the logic behind our collective accountability and be clear (and repetitive) as to what the accountability is and why. In doing so, we can help them own a sense of responsibility to themselves and not just to us, to the things for which they are accountable not just the fact of their accountability. The alternative of enforcing accountability is a perpetual grind. If, instead, we facilitate responsibility and have that rooted in powerful relationships, then accountability develops as a natural extension of it all.

For this to happen, we have to expose our logic and be transparent about our decision-making processes, vision, and expectations - which presumes, of course, that our practice is rooted in some sort of logic. If translatable logic is absent, it will be almost impossible to remain consistent, to communicate well, or to instill a sense of trust in others over time. Logic is the objective connection between the concepts of responsibility and accountability. This does not imply that ours is the correct logical connection or the only logical connection, just a transparent connection that is communicable and defensible. Think about it this way: imagine you are responsible for finding and creating operational efficiencies in your organization, but when it comes to performance review time, your manager holds you accountable for the sales quotas. There is no logical connection for you as it relates to things you have control of in your job, things you feel responsible for. Even if this example seems absurd, most of us have examples in our work and in our lives where we were held accountable for things we felt we had no control over and felt no responsibility for.

Alternately, many of us feel responsible for things for which we are never held accountable. When I worked in nonprofits, I was held accountable, mostly by funders, for short-term individual and community outcomes from our work, outcomes achieved in a given reporting period or grant cycle. Did our youth develop certain skills? Did a certain number of community members attend meetings? That kind of thing. I felt my deepest responsibility, however, for how we did our work, the day-to-day process and relationship building, and how that could sustain us over time, far beyond a grant cycle, and even beyond the life of our organization. Most funders didn't care how we worked as long as the outcomes met what we had proposed to receive their funding. My sense of personal responsibility simply took a longer view, and a more holistic view, than the people to whom I was accountable. Whether in a relationship to a funder or to an investor, this can be a recipe for destructive tension, particularly in early stages of work. It is a burden that transformative leaders must navigate and bear. We have to be out in front of the people we are accountable to and the things we are held accountable for. We need to lead from a place of responsibility. That's how we change things.

To do this through powerful relationships, we have to keep responsibility and accountability connected and clear in our minds. We have to personally understand, iterate on, and stay committed to the underlying logic of our work. We must embody and communicate to others that logic and how it will lead us toward our collective goals, so that they can feel our same sense of responsibility and accountability.

This is why clarity is so important. Clarity with logic is rooted in the ability to plainly answer the what, why, when, where, how, and for whom around any and all of our actions and decisions. While this may seem laborious or unreasonable, when our actions are rooted in our sense of responsibility and tied to our accountability, when there is an underlying logic connecting those, these elements and explanations are implicit in our decisions. So, articulating them to others with clarity does not require some deep new analysis but simply a deliberate communication effort. Being able to communicate clarity with ease and consistency is a further demonstration of our investment in our relationship with others. It builds trust. It's a show of respect. We seek clarity not to impose our logic on others in the form of coercion or compliance but to evoke a sense of ownership from others through their deeper understanding of our process. In doing so, we empower others. We invite them to question and challenge our logic, not just our outcomes, which can further empower all of us.

Appeal to Others' Logic (don't just impose yours)

We can't impose our logic, no matter how clearly we articulate it. We have to appeal to others and try to get them to understand and own it for themselves.

In 2011, I had the opportunity to help start the Tennessee College Access and Success Network to promote and invest in college access across the state and to increase the number of Tennesseans with a postsecondary degree. As part of our early efforts, we trained a cohort of local leaders around leading change in their schools and communities. We knew that bringing others into the work required a significant shift in traditional mindsets and expectations, not to mention practices; and we knew that we needed to meet people where they were. With this in mind, a colleague introduced the network (and me) to Social Judgment Theory. See Figure 4.

In this training, we were working with a group of early network members on how to think strategically about who could or should become college access supporters and advocates in our various communities and how we could start that conversation. What should outreach look like? What would be the best messaging? Of particular focus were those potential partners who were less obvious, not necessarily the progressive educators or known student champions. We considered janitors, receptionists, and other support staff in schools. We looked at community groups like Rotary Clubs or Chambers of Commerce. We talked about the local faith communities, local foundations, and other youth services organizations. For all of these potential partners, a critical mass of which would be required to build local momentum and investment in our work, we needed to message college access in a way they could hear and be motivated by.

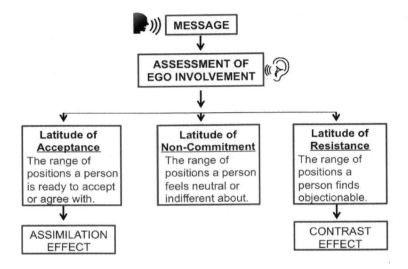

Social Judgment Theory lays out three domains that people fall into when receiving a message, whether about college access or anything else: 1. the latitude of resistance, 2. the latitude of non-commitment, or 3. the latitude of acceptance. In the latitude of resistance, our message contrasts with the recipients' frame of reference such that they reject it outright. In non-commitment, our message inspires no real response, either for or against. In the latitude of acceptance, our message reinforces the recipients' frame of reference such that they immediately agree with us. Any message we want to convey will fall into one of these latitudes because our audience will receive new information based on what they already know and/or feel about the topic, their frame of reference, their logic.

If we want our message to be received, to be in the latitude of acceptance, we have to adapt our messages more intentionally to tap into the logic of the recipient. For example, a message about building a college access coalition premised on social justice and addressing racial disparities in higher education may really resonate for the community organizer we want to get involved in the work. But, that message is probably not going to resonate with most Chambers of Commerce that are more interested in how college access could spur economic development in an area. In fact, such a social justice message, in my experience, can actually scare them away and shift them to the latitude of resistance. The Rotary Club may be specifically looking to volunteer or be mentors while youth services organizations may just be trying to reduce high school dropouts. They need to hear how aspiring to college can instill hope, vision, and a reason to stay in school. Social Judgment Theory tells us that if we want to engage others in our work, no matter what that work is, we must understand and communicate to their frame of reference.

Let's take a more general example for those of us who work in larger organizations. Let's say our company is going through a significant reorganization, shuffling staff around, eliminating some positions, making leadership changes. Often, the company develops one blanket message for the sake of consistency, which makes sense. We don't want to get caught looking like we aren't being honest, telling this department this and that department that. On the other hand, once we get into communicating in smaller groups, departments, divisions and the like, we should give managers the tools to speak specifically to what the reorganization really means to their people. Assuming this is a department or division we aren't firing a lot of people in or eliminating altogether, we want a message that will reduce tension, nervousness, fear and ideally even garner support for the effort. The triggers for these will likely be different depending on the department and the type of work. How we talk about the reorganization to specific audiences will determine if our veteran marketer resists and retrenches toward the way things have always been, or perhaps even foments discontent among peers; or if perhaps our mid-level manager in IT starts looking for another job. How we message to specific people or groups of people will largely determine if we develop resistors or partners in our change work.

Social Judgment Theory codifies these relative response options in terms of either assimilation or contrast effects. In other words, it's not just about if someone hears or understands a message. It's not just about whether it resonates with their frame of reference. It's about what they do with it once it is received. How do they react? How do they share it with others? How do they internalize it for themselves and their work? In the latitude of acceptance, people consume new information and begin to own it because it already naturally aligns with their frame of reference. This is the assimilation effect. In the latitude of rejection, the new information contradicts existing perspectives, beliefs, or perceptions. People tend not only to resist the message, but to actually double down on their current frame of reference in contrast, not only generating new resistance but also deepening the original contrary frame of reference. This is the contrast effect. Information that falls into the latitude of non-commitment simply goes nowhere. It triggers no feeling and a general sense of passiveness.

While I didn't know of Social Judgment Theory at the time, I ran into it in a big way when I first began organizing. Early on, we had a young, progressive principal at one of our main high schools who had supported our work engaging youth as advocates and organizers to improve schools. Over a year or so, our work had evolved, our understanding of the issues deepened, and our demands for change had become clearer. So, as our youth began to openly discuss the lack of adequate college counseling and the low expectations of students in our community to the School Board and anyone else who would listen, we were blind-sided by comments in the media by this same principal that we felt undermined the validity of the youth's work and research. We were hurt and angry and felt betrayed by someone who we thought was a staunch ally.

To make a long story short, she too felt hurt and betrayed by our group who she thought were her allies in helping reform her school. The message she had received through our advocacy was that her teachers didn't care and her school counselors weren't doing their jobs. She heard that she wasn't doing her job and her school was failing her students. As a result, she went straight into the contrast effect. Her undermining of us was, upon reflection, understandably defensive and intentional. Our group and this principal were aligned in our aspirations for more engaged students with higher aspirations and better prospects for college, but, we had failed miserably in our early messaging around that alignment.

105

After a facilitated heart-to-heart reflection with our team and the principal, we realigned and all got better at our work together. Our relationship was stronger than ever. She continued to be an outspoken advocate for what we were doing and we, in turn, were more aware of how our work and specifically our message could inadvertently negatively impact our greatest ally, and thus undermine the power of our work. Our work together ended up the subject of a documentary entitled "College on the Brain" in which this same principal was the central adult leader.

Whether we are trying to get someone to align around an advocacy effort, join a statewide college access network, or get behind an internal change initiative in our organization, we must understand their starting point or frame of reference on the issues at hand. If we do nothing else, we must try and keep our people out of a defensive posture, out of the latitude of resistance, and minimize the contrast effect. We have to keep some room to continue a conversation and explore common interests and avoid shutting down out of fear, confusion, or anything else. While this awareness and intentionality is critical in building relationships, it is often taken for granted once the relationships are in place. Sustaining powerful relationships requires that we treat even old relationships with the vigilance of the new, that we reflect and remain aware of how our messages and appeals to others can continue to support and grow our power rather than undermine it.

PART III.
Putting Power into Action

"The world isn't divided neatly into two classes of people, "the powerful" and "the powerless". Rather, people – particularly when acting in organized association with others, in coalitions and alliances – can access an incredible amount of unmobilized, unrealized or potential power...The starting point for all success is an unyielding belief that we can succeed, that we can make a difference."[11]

– Samuel Halperin

[11] Halperin, Samuel. "A Guide for the Powerless and Those Who Don't Know Their Own Power: A Primer on the American Political Process." *American Youth Policy Forum*: 9-10. Web.

As you might expect, putting power into action isn't just about what we do but also about *who* we are and *how* we are with others. Putting power into action starts with overcoming the limitations and powerlessness we have accepted within ourselves and within the relationships closest to us. As we liberate ourselves from these false constraints, we can bring others into the same process. We can then learn from their process of liberation. This is the groundwork of putting power into action – identifying and claiming our own power and helping others do the same. It has to start here. We can't expect to unearth the power of the mighty oak tree if we aren't willing to find the acorn, dig into the dirt a bit, water and care for it over time. The choice is ours to find our power, claim it, nurture it, and give it purpose – to commit over time to help it grow with others.

The following provides some recommendations for putting power into action in ways that will build and sustain powerful relationships and produce meaningful work over time.

Understand your own power.

If we are not aware of the nature of the power that we have, it becomes hard to avoid the corruptions to which any exercise of power is susceptible. If we are to understand our own practice, we need a clear understanding of the basis and practice of our power.[12]

- Howard Sercombe

I started this book with a broad analysis of power and an argument for how and why we should understand it better. We must not only see power around us, but understand the power within us. To know the power around us and to understand others' power, we must be deeply and critically observant. To know and understand our own power, we must be deeply humble. While humility is often misunderstood and wrongly associated with weakness or deference, research shows a strong correlation between humility and what most of us experience in powerful relationships. Ashley Merryman's research shows us that *"humility doesn't weaken leaders' authority. It gives them more flexibility in how they use their power."*[13]

Humility keeps us flexible and mindful that we have power and that everyone around us also has power; and that these two are in constant exchange with each other. In other words, humility requires that we understand our individual relationships through the prism of the concepts discussed in this book: privilege, oppression, personal power, positional power and so forth.

---

[12] Sercombe, Howard. *Youth work ethics*. London: SAGE, 2010. 123 Print.
[13] Merryman, Ashley. "Leaders are more powerful when they're humble." *The Washington Post.* 8 Dec. 2016: Web.

In powerful relationships, knowing ourselves is as much about understanding others as it is anything else. We are no different than those around us. In the folksy wisdom of Myles Horton: *"You cannot move from where you ain't. You've got to move from where you are."*[14] Knowing where we are starts with understanding our own power. Obviously, we aren't seeking to understand power as some academic exercise or as if evaluating some static concept. We seek to understand our power so that we may transform it.

Use your power to transform power.

The Alternatives to Violence Project lays out "Guides to Transforming Power" that I have used for years when discussing this topic. I share them here with some of my own editorializing because the basic guides speak for themselves, and they speak better than I.

Seek to resolve conflicts by reaching for common ground.

Finding common ground reinforces the concepts of Social Judgment Theory related to understanding people's point of reference and communicating with people in light of that point of reference. If we don't start by reaching for common ground, then we often make our conflicts worse. When we advocate positions that are already in others' latitude of resistance, we give them even more reason to intensify the contrast effect and retrench in theirs. We push them further away from us and, more importantly, the work we are trying to accomplish. Notably, this guide says to "reach" for

---

[14] Horton, Myles, and Dale Jacobs. *The Myles Horton reader: education for social change*. Knoxville: U of Tennessee Press, 2003. 62. Print.

common ground and not the more familiar notion of *finding* common ground. Clearly, we want to find common ground but I think the notion of reaching for it as the goal is a way of connecting with others more genuinely even when common ground is difficult to find. Reaching is about good process, which in and of itself can lower levels of resistance.

Reach for what is good in others.

Reaching for the good in others is the ultimate manifestation of power as love. While it is important for people to feel confident and to hear positive feedback on some action they have taken, praising someone is not the same as reaching for what is good in them. When we reach for what is good in others, we have the opportunity to help them reach for what is good in themselves. We must reach for good in their core concept of themselves and not just individual actions they have taken. Like reaching for common ground, reaching for what is good in others shows them a process, an effort, of unpacking their own identity and assumptions about themselves and others. It delivers the value of positive reinforcement and models the process of reaching for it. This is in many ways the bigger transformation than just finding and delivering the good message. When others see and acknowledge the good in us, we look harder for it in ourselves. We allow ourselves the room to be proud of who we are. We give ourselves the opportunity to build on the parts of ourselves we value and others value, which leads us to more powerful relationships.

Listen before making judgments.

If we can't listen, we can't have a relationship. If we can't build a relationship, we can't transform power. If we think our power comes from being authoritative or from judging people then we see power only as something to be claimed, something individual. Just listening to others grows collective power. The trust that develops through good listening and communicating allows us a safer space for more critical, purposeful dialogue and action. In contrast, judgment without listening shuts people down and often puts people in the latitude of resistance triggering the contrast effect.

Base your position on truth.

When I use the "Guides to Transforming Power" in workshops, I always highlight this guide explicitly in tandem with the next because for so many of us they seem potentially contradictory, or at least counterintuitive. Basing our position on truth could imply that there is a clear and persistent truth. But, the next guide prompts us to be ready to revise our positions (which are still based in truth). Our truth is not always fact. So, this guide is really about basing our positions on the truth as we understand it, with the assumption that we will continue to learn and grow and revise our truth over time - a humble truth.

Be ready to revise your position if it is wrong.

In other words, our truth may end up being wrong and the position we staked on it may too. Alternately, our truth could remain but our interpretation of it and our related position on an issue may change. Either way, we must be self-aware enough to recognize and revise. As I've stated, transforming power requires humility. The power of humility is in the model it provides to others, a model of revising over righteousness, learning over knowing, of sharing power over claiming it, of we over I. My open acceptance of being wrong rather than reducing my power actually expands my power as it demonstrates my investment in our collective power.

Risk being creative rather than being violent.

The work of Robert Fritz, which I discuss more thoroughly in *Creating Matters*, challenges us to move from a problem-centric view of the world to a creative one. When we seek perpetually to solve problems, often problems rooted in some sort of violence, institutional or interpersonal, we remain rooted in that violence and the rules and understanding of the world that manifest and perpetuate it. To transform power, we have to create new rules. We have to understand and question and dismantle the norms and systems that create and sustain violent power structures and the problems we experience from those. We must have the courage and creativity to create a new order built on our vision, not merely to get past our current problem, which only prepares us to move to the next one.

Use surprise and humor.

Transforming power first requires us to be open and honest with ourselves and the world. This is often difficult work and can leave us feeling vulnerable. It can be emotional, painful work that can trigger a natural tendency within us to become defensive or retrench in the perceived safety of the status quo. Better the devil you know, as the saying goes. Surprise and humor are critical, tactical tools to help shift us from those positions and open us to the difficult, transformative work we are called to do. When we are dysfunctionally protecting ourselves from dealing with pain or even protecting others, surprise and humor can knock us out of our protective shell just enough to see it for what it is. They can help us move the work without being overwhelmed by the burden.

Be patient and persistent.

Transform is just another word for change. In powerful relationships, we are changing ourselves and helping others to do the same. We are changing our relationships. We ultimately aspire to change the systems that impact our lives in negative ways. This is a lot of change, and change is difficult. Change is confusing and emotional. Most people don't like change. Or, they are accepting of the idea of change but resistant to the actual process. So, we must have patience with ourselves and others. Grace. But, we also must be persistent. Urgency.

Build community based on honesty, respect, and caring.

Honesty, respect, and caring reinforce the concepts of trust and transparency that I have already discussed as fundamental to anyone seeking to build powerful relationships. We believe in community because we understand that community is the mechanism for transforming and expanding power with and through others. Building a strong and purposeful community is the ultimate strategy for delivering powerful work.

Understand what you want to change.

When we think about change, we often initially think about people we want to change. We want to change the neighbor who has different political beliefs. We want to change the colleague who does shoddy work. We want to change the elected official who introduced the offensive policy.

We can't and we won't change people. People change themselves. And, if we reflect on our own lives and where and how we have changed, it's typically because of an experience or a circumstance or a relationship that by its nature helped us think and act differently, helped us know ourselves and our world a little differently. A powerful relationship. A transformative relationship. So, when we talk about change, we need to be clear about our target. We have to think in terms of systems and parts of systems in which individuals can change themselves. Figure 4 provides a highly simplified, but useful, way of thinking about levels of change and the related effort and investment required to bring them about.

Are we asking people to develop new skills? Are we creating new processes and procedures in our group or organization that they will have to adapt to? Is the change structural and requiring major shifts in formal and informal relationships and power dynamics within the group or organizational? Are we attempting to change our culture and unearthing and undoing unspoken norms and behaviors that have never been questioned? It's important to understand that cultural change will require structural, procedural, and skills changes in support of it. Each of these levels of change has a sort of nested relationship with the levels below them.

116

Figure 4: Type of Change versus Magnitude[15]

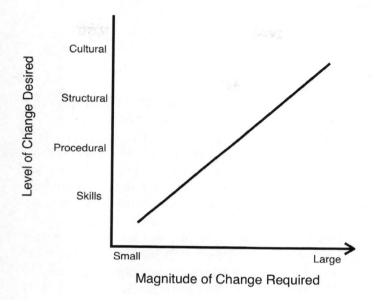

In addition to working on college access, my youth and I did some organizing and advocacy around the issue of predatory lending in our community: payday loans, title loans, refund anticipation loans, and the like. All of these loans are targeted at people in a cash crisis and hook them into a perpetual cycle of high interest debt. Emotionally, we wanted those businesses out of our community. But, as we explored the issue more deeply, things got a lot more complicated.

We wanted to stop businesses that were raking in hundreds of millions of dollars from the working poor.

---

[15] Adapted from the work of the Adler Group

117

At the same time, the working poor often do have short-term cash needs. Sadly, however, those who visit a predatory lender end up with perpetual cash needs as they remain in a cycle of cash crises taking out one loan to pay off another. This, by the way, is why we see so many payday loan places clustered together in low-income communities.

So, my youth and I had to think about the real-world needs and practices of people in our community who visited these places. We started with community education workshops to try to raise awareness and build new skills around financial management, budgeting, and the like. We realized we had a crisis at the lowest level of change – basic *skills* and awareness. In developing new skills, however, we had to provide and connect people with new outlets for better financial management – new *procedures* for managing their cash flow. We had to work with banks to get more people into banking relationships and work with the unbanked to try to convince them that it was okay to turn their money over to an institution rather than keep it in their mattress. We set up free tax preparation workshops focused on helping people claim the Earned Income Tax Credit and expediting the tax filing and return process – while promoting getting a bank account for an auto deposit of their return. We wanted to keep them out of paying fees for simple tax preparation and at least reduce the need for refund anticipation loans by narrowing the window of time between submission and receipt of a return.

As the advocacy effort continued, however, we realized that the scope and scale of changing policies (structural changes) and cultural changes – reducing the demand while providing more opportunities- were bigger than us. We needed lobbyists to counter the payday lending industry's lobbyists, and that wasn't going to happen from our little youth organization. We ultimately passed leadership of this work on to more sustainable, broader reaching, adult-led organizations and took on a partnership role. We had to be honest about the levels of change we wanted to achieve and adjust our role and strategy toward those ends. Again, it wasn't about us or our organization; it was about the work.

Because of my experiences like these in working with youth, I have also had the opportunity to write and consult for years around more student-centric schools. Unfortunately, this work was often unable to align around the levels of systemic changes that I would have hoped for. If I evaluate some of these consulting experiences through the levels of change in Figure 4, the challenges of this change work make more sense.

To start, there are very few people who will openly say that they don't think that students should be engaged in school, so it seems like this is pretty promising ground and a good opportunity for helping transform the learning environment in schools. On this promise, my colleagues and I have trained teachers around creating more engaging and democratic classrooms. We've trained students to support deeper engagement in learning. We have helped teachers and students develop new *skills*. We have helped teachers with processes and *procedures* to facilitate the practice of listening to students and engaging them in their classes. And, more times than not, this is where our work on a given engagement ends.

At another time, we may have a different body of work with another client with a similar vision around student engagement. This time, we work with a school district and help them define the vision and identify the policies, standards, and *structural* shifts that have to take place to make student engagement a reality. We talk about building more engaging and inclusive cultures and more supportive school climates. Perhaps we provide some procedures for how to monitor school culture and climate. And, more times than not, this is where that particular engagement ends.

In the first body of work, we worked with the "front line" of change. We hopefully imparted some new skills and procedures for engaging students but often left them working in an organizational structure and culture that systemically didn't support this same vision of student engagement. They had new tools but they were still working against the structural and cultural grain. In the second body of work, we worked from the top down, but never addressed the "down" part. We left leadership with the tools to direct high-level change around structures and culture but never instilled the skills and procedures at the front line to actually implement them. So, their efforts end up looking detached from the front-line realities of their staff.

In either case, the level of change we were able to invest in did not meet the level of change at least theoretically desired. Changing and developing new skills is relatively easy and can be quite fast. Changing cultures is much more difficult and occurs over years, even generations perhaps. The whole of these efforts need to be more aligned and invested in over a longer period of time than most of our contracts were designed for. This is not to say that our work was meaningless or fruitless or otherwise a failure. It was just part of a larger change process – a process that needed to be owned and sustained long after we left, and usually by a lot more people than we actually had access to. Our clients needed to build their own creative tension with their people and often too much of that creative tension relied on us.

I realize that understanding change just in terms of level and magnitude is pretty theoretical. It's a framework for organizing our thinking, not really putting change into action. So, when we are working and organizing and leading every day, we need a more practical understanding of what we are trying to change, and, by default, what we are not. We need tools to help us focus our work. Early and often in my career I have come back to a simple process I learned called "Exploding the Issue" which seems to have originated from a group called Need in Deed. It's a simple visualization that could be done on an individual sheet of paper, or as a group process on butcher paper on the wall – which is how I typically did it.

It starts with identifying a problem statement. So, for us for example, that could have been: "Only 1 in 10 students at our school will make it to college." I'm actually pretty sure we did that one a few times over the years. As an aside, I also used this process less formally with one young woman who was having issues with her mom at home. In our conversational version of "Exploding the Issue", her problem statement was something about her mom yelling at her or slamming doors or something to that effect. The process works on all levels to objectify the problem and our experience of it.

With the problem statement in the middle of the page or spread on the wall, we brainstormed what some of the symptoms were of that problem and wrote them above the problem statement. See Figure 5. For the college access problem, symptoms could have included unemployment, low wages, low motivation, students dropping out of high school, crime, and even gangs. The process is additive, so this is not the time to refute others, but allow people to explain their logic and make connections between their experiences and the problem. After brainstorming the symptoms, we switched to brainstorming the causes. We wrote them below the problem statement. Again, for the college access issue, this could be low expectations, teachers who didn't understand their students, a lack of college counselors, students not knowing they could go to college, family fears of their child leaving them, and so forth. Some of the symptoms and causes can be the same by the way. Many of these problems are, in fact, cycles, so the symptoms and the causes can be one and the same. Again, the process is additive, so don't worry about it being "right" but just defensible. From the causes, we can even drill down to root causes like racism, classism, poverty, and the like, which allows for a much broader and less strategic conversation, but a critical one for framing and understanding our work nonetheless.

The point of this process is to help identify a reasonable target for action and a deeper understanding of what the issue really looks like. For our work, this process helped us focus on the issue of college access from two directions: first, reaching out to students to help them know they could go to college and that they should be demanding support from their schools in the process; and secondly, advocating for not only more guidance counselors in schools but dedicated college counselors. Whenever we felt lost in the work, we could come back to this simple process of exploding the issue and re-ground ourselves and check where we were targeting our resources and action.

Figure 5: Exploding the Issue

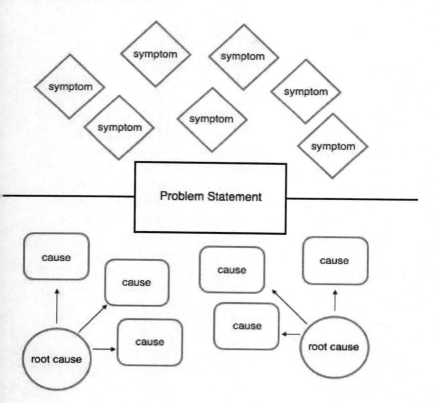

Understand change itself.

There are volumes of work on this subject, so I won't pretend to try and give the whole topic its due. I will, however, focus on a couple of frameworks I have returned to repeatedly over the years to help people see change in a different way; mostly to help them objectify their often negative experiences with it.

Change only begins when something ends. The work of William Bridges crystallizes the process of change in a way that, for me, was a real a-ha. See Figure 6. Beginning the Transition Curve model with an "ending" allows us to make sense of some of the emotional impact and reaction we get in response to change efforts. From initial denial, anger, and shock, we only slide further into fear and anger and so forth. Passing through these stages gets us to what Bridges calls the "ditch of doubt" where we just avoid the change altogether. Much like the "Exploding the Issue" example, this Transition Curve can be very personal in nature or could be used to understand community or organizational change in the aggregate. The framework holds even as the lived process is nonlinear and the timeline for getting through it is as individual as the people experiencing the change. I recently shared Bridges' work with someone who had been through a very difficult divorce and was wondering why she wasn't "over it" yet. It had been less than a year. In reality, she was probably still just on the upside of the ditch of doubt.

Change is no different than most of the ideas in this book: it typically happens through and with people and in relationships among people and contexts. It is impacted by our awareness of power - our own and others'. Change is complicated by all of the nuances that make each of us who we are as individuals. We have to understand and deal with this process of change first through the complexity of our humanity, not just in terms of the systems that surround us. We have to see how dealing with change happens in the "I", "you", and "we" domains as well as in the systemic and structural domains.

Figure 6: The Transition Curve

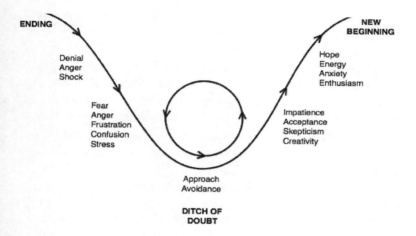

If we can understand where we are as individuals in navigating change as well as where we are in our relationships, then we have a better chance of understanding how our organizations and other broader networks of relationships are navigating change. We can move our discussion of change as something individual and deeply personal to one that is more strategic and about the work we are trying to accomplish. To this end, there is an interesting and deceptively simple change model out of Harvard:

$$Change = Dissatisfaction \times Vision \times Plan$$

Why is this simple model so powerful? At the basic level, what happens when we have a zero for any of these elements? No change.

It's basic multiplication, but also profound in that so many of our traditional organizational change efforts are built on addition strategies. If we do this and then we get that then it will add up to change. If we add this resource...If we add this position...If we add this new frame for our work...add this plan and so forth.

Addition alone doesn't generate real change. Change is multiplicative. The elements necessary for change are interdependent and exponential magnifiers of each other. If we want to generate change, we must understand the whole concept. We must invest the time, energy, and effort to turn dissatisfaction into creative tension, to use it to build a shared vision, and capture it in a plan to deliver the change we collectively want and need. Most of us have experienced more visioning sessions and created more plans than we care to admit. Organizations and consultants churn these things out with the intent of marking guideposts to spur change efforts. And yet, most of these visioning sessions and plans haven't generated the types of changes we needed or hoped for when we started them.

Given the Harvard model, the obvious implication, which may seem counterintuitive, is that to generate change we may have to invest in cultivating more dissatisfaction. Sometimes that's what is required to build sufficient support and energy for a new vision and plan to implement it. Dissatisfaction is something we possess individually and it is a state we usually want out of, so it taps our individual motivation to change.

The sort of dissatisfaction I am promoting here, however, should not be confused with the unfocused, undirected dissatisfaction that cuts at the core of many group and organizational cultures, the sort of dissatisfaction that often results in finger-pointing and blame and back-stabbing. This sort of dissatisfaction is obviously a form of destructive tension; and while it often generates the desire for change, it is usually the expectation that someone else needs to do the changing.

To transition to a form of dissatisfaction that may drive positive change and generate creative tension, we need to find opportunities for more shared responsibility and accountability for our work. After all, it's easy to point at and be dissatisfied with others when we don't have a powerful relationship with them or share ownership in the same work. It's also really easy in this case to do nothing. When we do share responsibility and accountability, however, we have a different motivation to change skills, procedures, and even structures that are preventing us from delivering on our shared goals.

To drive group and organizational change, we need to value and cultivate what Francesca Gina calls "constructive nonconformity" which she defines as "behavior that deviates from organizational norms, others' actions, or common expectations, to the benefit of the organization."[16] Implied in the idea of constructive nonconformity is that our people, not just us, become more aware of the cultural norms that protect the status quo. We all must be aware of and able to surface,

---

[16] "Let Your Workers Rebel" Harvard Business Review,
https://hbr.org/cover-story/2016/10/let-your-workers-rebel

articulate, and critique our organizational patterns and behaviors. We must be keen observers of our own and others' actions and have safe avenues for critical, constructive feedback. We must cultivate our group or organizational culture as a living, future-oriented concept, not as a backward-looking summation of how things are and how they got there. We need to facilitate cultures in which destructive conformity, deference, and apathy become the real transgressions while healthy dissatisfaction, creativity, and stoking meaningful change become openly celebrated.

Work intergenerationally.

Depending on the magnitude of change we are seeking, change can take from a few hours (skill development) to decades (culture change). The work that laid the foundation for Rosa Parks' transformative action had begun decades before by A. Phillip Randolph and countless others. The shifts that we have seen more recently in support for LGBT rights and specifically marriage equality seems to have happened relatively quickly, unless we look closer at the generations before who worked in isolation and often in direct danger to bring these issues to the collective consciousness. The evolution in perspective here is generational, with younger generations incrementally less rooted in past cultural norms. This is the longitudinal reality of culture change. Each new generation comes into the world with a baseline knowledge of the world and expectations premised on the changes made by the previous generations. Perhaps the most obvious and pronounced example of this is that anyone under the age of 8 at the time of this writing has never known an America where a black American could never become President. In terms of memory, it's probably more like anyone under the age of 12 or 13.

This simple reality demonstrates why younger people aren't inevitably rooted in the problems of the past. Their vision and hope and ideals can inspire and liberate older generations who may be more cautious or jaded from that past. On the other hand, it means younger generations can also be blindsided by the persistence of those problems in more nuanced forms in the present and future. Their naiveté, so to speak, is both an asset and a potential challenge. Adults' historical knowledge and experience can be the same.

So, working across generations is not only smart but explicitly necessary to see large scale change come to fruition. We need the mix of energy and naiveté and experience and jadedness to balance and inform our work in the present. We also need to make sure the work doesn't fade as older generations move on and pass on. In other words, this isn't just about preparing to "pass the torch" to the next generation sometime in the future, but rather about expanding the flame in the present. Remember, Martin Luther King Jr. was still practically a youth when he claimed the mantle of Civil Rights Movement leadership. John Lewis was still in his late teens and early twenties. By the late 1950's and early 1960's, A. Phillip Randolph and others from a previous generation knew that this moment would be and should be owned and led by young people. The older generation knew that their role was in support and training and leveraging long-built networks, but was not to be the figurehead leaders of the new Movement. It was good strategy to step back and let young people be the more visible leaders.

To be clear, working across generations is not the easiest way to work. It is the strategic way to work. We have to be willing as adults to be open to new perspectives and passions of younger people. We need to validate and embrace these. We can't be the gatekeepers of the work forcing younger people to adopt solely to our ways or be left out of the work. We have to be bridge builders, inviting new pathways and perspectives. Alternately, young people have to be open and willing to learn from our experiences, to partner with us with respect for the work and time and experiences we have put in over years. In our organizations or networks, we must be willing to slow down and take the time to build intergenerational relationships.

Southern Echo in Mississippi is considered one of the national experts on intergenerational work. It was founded by Civil Rights Movement veteran Hollis Watkins who started his activism in the 1960's as a youth, and now works and serves in the adult role working in partnership with youth. Southern Echo has documented some key concepts around intergenerational work:

1. (Intergenerational means) bringing younger and older people together in the work on the same basis.

2. (Intergenerational means) enabling younger and older people to develop the skills and tools of organizing work and leadership development, side by side, so that in the process they can learn to work together, learn to respect each other, and overcome the fear and suspicion of each that is deeply rooted in the culture.

3. (Intergenerational work requires us) to create a learning process and a work strategy that ensure that younger people develop the capacity to do the work without being intimidated, overrun or outright controlled by the older people in the group. "Control" and "exercise of authority" are great temptations for older people, even for those who have long been in the struggle and strongly believe in the intergenerational model.

Southern Echo makes it clear that we have to be deeply invested in the strategy of working across generations and describes the deep philosophical roots necessary to do it well. The third point, in particular, directly addresses the challenges of sharing power intergenerationally. We have to acknowledge and address the reality that young people are often taught to defer power to adults while adults are conditioned to claim power and use it as authority. Clearly, to work together, these habits and norms must be disrupted. This is a complicated process, so I have developed a few more specific critical factors of my own to support and contextualize intergenerational work:

Keys to Intergenerational Work
1. There must be a goal that neither adults nor young people can achieve, or achieve as well, on their own.
2. Effective, empowered young people are a core strategy for achieving collective goals.
3. Effective, empowered adults share power and support and create space for young people to lead.

4. Youth and adults work as a team with differing and complementary skills, personal networks, perspectives, and opportunities to lead.
5. Both youth and adults share responsibility and accountability for the collective work and achieving shared goals.

If you see strong parallels among the keys to intergenerational work and our discussion of creative tension earlier, it's because it was my own intergenerational work that helped crystalize creative tension for me.

Objectify the work, but never the people.

It is very easy to objectify someone who sees or understands the world differently than we do on a given issue. I am as guilty of it as anyone. We fall into simple and absurd generalizations. The opposite political party is ideological, foolish, and short sighted. People who need a little help are "takers" who live off the hard work of the wealthy, the "makers". Anyone who is wealthy exploits the poor. The police don't like black people; black people hate the police. We are so entrenched in positions rather than dialogue or learning that we not only objectify others, but in doing so objectify ourselves. We can't share power, transform power, or build powerful relationships with objects, as objects.

This sort of objectification of the other is pretty obvious and yet insidious. Equally dangerous and less obvious, however, is how we objectify ourselves and those closest to us in more subtle but potentially destructive ways. When we work on important issues, personal issues, we can get lost in our own stories and in the beauty and pain and triumph of the stories of those with whom we are working. This is particularly true when we are working to change difficult social, cultural, or economic conditions, working with and against issues of privilege and oppression. When we are trying to create change like this, our stories are what bring us to the work, what bring us together. Anecdotes and moving personal tales inspire us. They motivate us. But, they can also get in our way.

When we decide we want to change something bigger than ourselves, we must be committed to the fact that it isn't about us anymore – except in as much as we can be powerful and strategic parts of the larger effort. So, we have to take those personal experiences and externalize them, de-personalize them. We have to objectify them as stories, turn them into data or examples of why we are doing the work we are doing. We have to try to universalize them to better understand and communicate broader conditions and how they impact and relate to others. My story should become symbolic or representative of the stories of others struggling with the same issues. We use stories as a tool for bringing others into the work.

Some people struggle with using personal stories this way. They feel it cheapens the individual experience or otherwise capitalizes on someone's potentially painful reality. For some, it feels exploitative. And, it can be. But, the reality is that when done well, this is part of the process of turning presumed powerlessness into power. The story of the powerless can be an extraordinary spark for change, the power implicit in personal experience, in finding one's own voice.

We have to navigate our stories and our potential traumas carefully and with due respect for ourselves and others. We don't want to inadvertently trigger someone's suffering, to make them relive their traumas, while they stand behind a microphone trying to mobilize a crowd, or stand in front of their colleagues trying to inspire them to engage their work. We want them and their stories to be powerful, not exploitative. Exploitation usurps power. So, we have to be smart about how and where and what part of our stories we share.

I remember a young woman I worked with many years back who was living in very difficult circumstances. Housing projects. Addicted mother and sister. Drug dealers making home deliveries and spending too much time just hanging around. Violence all around, inside and outside of her home. One day when it was clear that all of this was taking its toll on her, I offered my help in just listening initially. She was tough, so she kind of blew me off. So, I persisted wanting her to know I was there for her. And finally, she stopped me and said: "Thanks, Anderson. I appreciate it. I know you'll listen. But, today I just want to work." This was one of the biggest lessons of my career and inadvertently validated our approach to engaging youth in the work that mattered to them. What she was telling me was: today, I don't want to be defined by my problems, an object of my circumstances. I want to focus on working to change them. I want that to be who I am today, the version of me with dreams and aspirations and motivation. I want and need that power. She deserved that power.

Her personal story drove not only her work but motivated others as well. She had credibility. She was living near the worst of what our community could offer. She was an example for our team, our Board, our funders, and our advocacy, not only of what we were working against but of what we could become by doing this work together. She accepted this, and owned her role as an evangelist over several years of work, even as a teenager. And yet, on this day, and certainly others, she needed to step away from that story, the one where she was largely a victim, and focus on a new one she was actively crafting where she was the victor over her circumstances. She needed to objectify her story and work on behalf of other people who live in poverty, deal with violence and so forth. It didn't need to be, and at times, couldn't be about her, her poverty, her victimization. It was too personal, even potentially debilitating.

As this work evolved, we learned about and talked more and more about the concept of "strategic sharing" developed by Casey Family Programs as a way to make sure we own and share our stories in a safe, purposeful way, a way to make sure we don't objectify ourselves or each other. It's a way to protect and grow our power with others, and not just give it away. Strategic sharing is all about making good choices about how we tell our life stories so that our voices can be heard while our wellbeing is protected. As I've noted, at its best, sharing from personal experience can educate, inspire, and make a real difference in our work. Stories are memorable and compelling; they put a human face on issues, needs, and triumphs. Disclosing too much personal information, however, also carries some risks. Sharing personal experiences can make us vulnerable and may make our listeners unproductively uncomfortable.

Before we share, we need to ask ourselves and plan what we will share and what we want to keep private. We need to be able to answer: 1. What is my purpose in sharing this information about myself or my family? 2.

Who benefits from my sharing this information? and 3. What is it that I want the audience to learn or gain from it?

To be able to answer these questions then, we also have to know our audience. This will help guide some of our choices. It also helps to know deeply about the issues that are part of our story, so we can draw the line between our story and more general knowledge, say, about violence in the home, or discrimination, or education. We need the knowledge and tools to jump into statistics or more general insights when we feel ourselves getting too deep into our personal narrative, risking over sharing. We need to be in control of what and when and why we share.

My father committed suicide. This is part of my story. Some days I can share it with clear eyes and a strong voice and some days it can be really difficult, even linger for hours or days in my head and heart. I know this because I have paid attention to what sharing this information does to me and I measure it against why I share it in the first place. I share this part of my personal story because I know that others who have similar experiences with suicide, sexual abuse, and Depression are afraid to talk about it. So, even when it's tough on me, I feel powerful in being willing and able to share. It is strategic and is shared with a deep sense of purpose and commitment that I developed watching my Dad suffer, and then watching and listening to the responses, or lack thereof, to his suicide. Again, speaking about my Dad's struggles and suicide has given power and strategic purpose to one of the most powerless feeling times of my life because I am in control of how and when I talk about it. I can make it personal and about me or my Dad or I can de-personalize it and make it about Depression and suicide.

It is admittedly ironic that a process of de-personalization is actually what can keep us from objectifying ourselves and others. As we build networks and put our power into action, we need to apply this same process of de-personalization to the potential partners or targets of our work, including the systems and structures we are trying to change. This thinking can be summarized by one of Dr. King's Principles of Nonviolence: Nonviolence seeks to defeat injustice, not people. Nonviolence recognizes that evil-doers are also victims of unjust systems and not evil people.[17] In other words, to objectify and focus our work on the changes we desire, we have to avoid objectifying our perceived opposition as individuals. Our understanding of our work must be systemic and we must avoid getting distracted by too much focus on one or more individuals – even though these individuals often do the most to incite our deep emotions and sense of injustice.

As part of this effort, it's helpful to map our networks as a group exercise to visualize where we might invest our time and energy to most effectively build our power. We can start by brainstorming all of the individuals we know who would relate positively or negatively to the issue we are trying to change. Then, we can brainstorm the groups, organizations, institutions, or other formal entities we are connected with. This should just be a big messy individual and group brainstorm. All of the individual members of the group should put those names up on sticky notes on a wall so everyone can see them, and you can still move them around. We need to

---

[17] http://www.thekingcenter.org/king-philosophy

see collectively all of the people we know and organizations we might work with. We need to see how exponentially bigger our networks are together so that we can get a visual sense of our collective potential power.

On the other hand, just because we know someone doesn't mean that they are interested or engaged in what we are trying to accomplish on a given set of work. Just because someone is a friend of ours doesn't mean they are a friend of our work, or this particular work. Just because someone may not be interested in this particular work also doesn't mean they are not a friend or not a partner for future work. We have to be honest about this. Again, we have to think strategically, not personally. With our network brainstorm of individuals and organizations, we can take this analysis a step further and map them along a spectrum, from opposition on one hand to ally on the other. The Spectrum of Allies is a tool used almost everywhere in my organizing experience, but I'm not sure of its original source. See Figure 7. Again, this is where we need to be honest and objective. The people around us, friends, family, teachers, co-workers, faith community, and so on, all fit somewhere in our spectrum of allies. Their placement doesn't change how much we like or love or trust them. We just need to be honest about who we can and need to reach out to to join us and who, despite being a friend or colleague, simply isn't going to be there for us on this one.

Once we map our spectrum of allies, we can have a more critical conversation about which of those relationships along the spectrum have the most potential to impact our work, positively or negatively. We need to evaluate our time, energy, skills, and other resources and focus on individuals and organizations who will drive

Figure 7: Spectrum of Allies

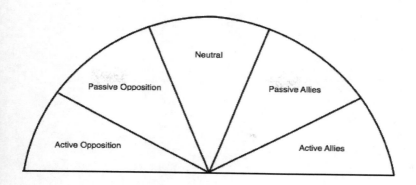

the biggest impact based on what we have to invest in bringing them into the work. To do this as another group exercise, we can actually transition our spectrum to a power analysis visual like the one presented in Figure 8. This will allow us to assess not only the degree to which someone may be inclined to support our work but also how much power they may have to make things happen. Clearly, for example, there is no need to invest resources in people or organizations who fall in the active opposition/less power quadrant. Additionally, there's not much use in investing time and resources into the active ally/less power quadrant. You get the idea. This is all about further focusing where we will invest our time and resources to get the most return.

While it may seem odd that we didn't just start with this visual to begin with, it's important for us to brainstorm our networks without the potential to explicitly or implicitly include or exclude people based on our perception of their power. Power analysis is a separate discussion and a good network brainstorm and spectrum of allies should leave us with as much raw material as possible to consider as a starting point, or even milepost, for our work.

Figure 8: Power Analysis

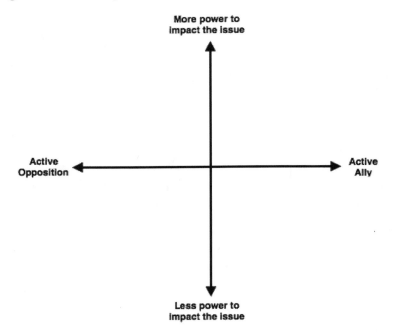

Without mapping our networks and having critical strategy and resource conversations in this way, we run the risk of either spending too much time with our allies or too many resources trying to win over our entrenched, active opposition. The people and organizations in the poles of the spectrum are the ones who have the potential to kill the work, albeit for very different reasons. The most intense opposition will consume our resources even as they incite our greatest passions and emotions. We think that they are the "big fish" and if we can just catch them then our work will be done. We rarely catch those fish, particularly before we put a lot of time and effort into strengthening our base of smaller fish. We can easily burn ourselves out and expend undo resources in the belief that we might change our most active opposition.

On the other hand, we can also spend too much time with our active allies. To extend the metaphor, this is sort of like shooting fish in a barrel. It's too easy. It's distracting and too much time with our closest allies can make us think we are being more effective than we really are. We must beware of groupthink and too much vigorous head nodding that make it seem like we've built more power than we actually have. We need to mobilize our allies, but not always be surrounded by them.

If we are working our personal and group networks strategically, we will likely focus on the people and organizations in the middle of the spectrum with the most power to impact the work. This is where we will find our initial returns on time and energy and relationship investments. We need to evaluate and try to understand their perspectives, why they might be opposed, for, or ambivalent about our work. Is there a part of the work in particular that would resonate? In some cases this could mean that they have some interest in the topic or issue and in others we may have enough personal power that our just reaching out is enough to generate at least initial buy in. We need to treat each of these efforts at early outreach uniquely and with this level of intentionality. This again underscores the previous discussion about Social Judgment Theory and the need to understand as much as possible about our potential allies' frame of reference. Over time, we can revisit this process and our spectrum will become more clear and more accurate, which in most cases, is more important than it just showing a larger network. Most importantly, we can hopefully show how we have moved people toward being active allies from wherever they started on the spectrum.

Use your power creatively.

Creativity is the power to connect the seemingly unconnected.
                                                    - William Plomer

Freedom Rider and fellow Nashvillian Rip Patton often talks about the strategy of "dramatizing the issue" as core to their work in the Movement and still critical to social change efforts he still leads today. In doing so, he highlights the fundamental and strategic creativity, rarely given its due, of the Civil Rights Movement. The silent marches. The simplicity and symbolism of sitting-in at a lunch counter. The nonviolence. Patton's and his peer's ability to dramatize the issue of segregation in a way that new audiences could see, understand, and even feel it was critical to their ultimate success. This included creatively leveraging the media and understanding the power of images. Despite the social and political institution of segregation, the moral underpinnings of it were extremely fragile. And, when they put segregation and the violence of the state on display, the children of the Movement started to awaken a common sense of morality amongst previously passive citizens all over the country. How could they do that to these children? How could they use attack dogs and bully clubs and water hoses on peaceful protests? What was so offensive about sitting at a counter and wanting a soda anyway? What was so wrong with riding on a bus? How could any of this warrant the violence they were seeing on television and in newspapers?

The children of the Civil Rights Movement found a new way to tell an old story, new tools to make an old case for civil rights. Part of their success was timing and built on the backs of generations before, but part was also rooted in the creative acts of nonviolent revolution. As we discussed earlier, there was power in what they didn't do, how they didn't retaliate. They did not engage segregation on its terms but rather on the terms of their vision of a Beloved Community. In the end, violence isn't all that creative.

I remember riding back from one of our partner high schools early in my work in youth organizing feeling a bit demoralized and wondering how we could wake people up to the fact that our students wanted and deserved the opportunity to go to college. I had been doing my own research on the topic, reading white papers from think tanks from across the political spectrum. It was all pretty boring. It all made the same case we were trying to make but who really cared about another white paper or batch of research from some think tank? They weren't in Nashville. They didn't know "these" students or "our" schools or neighborhood issues. The research was too distant even if it resonated with the general state of things in our schools and community. Then, it dawned on me: our youth should write their own white paper! What if we engaged the

143

issue based on our vision of youth leadership and justice rather than getting trapped problem by problem in the broken system? What's the last thing anyone would expect from a group of students from "failing" schools, who many don't expect to graduate, and pretty much no one thinks will, or even wants to go to college? A well-researched, student-led, student written white paper on the issue of college access in their schools.

My youth spent almost a year and a half learning how to research, researching, making presentations, writing, advocating for funding all while preparing the white paper. By the time it was complete, no one in the city knew more about college access than these youth. To this day, I believe the surprise (recall the use of surprise in transforming power) of the white paper and the students' expertise on the topic, combined with their personal stories to make it all real, are what opened us to many new critical allies. This work ultimately led to the creation of the first college access center in the city for first generation students.

Whether we are helping others discover their power or helping institutions change how they deploy theirs, we must think and act creatively in order to disrupt old thinking, present new possibilities, and invite people into the work. Sometimes, we have to tell old stories in new ways. Sometimes, we have to present new stories to old audiences. Sometimes we don't know what we need to do, but we have a grave sense of urgency to do something. Regardless, how creative we are in approaching the work will be directly mirrored by the nature and breadth of relationships we are able to build to drive and sustain the work.

Always question power.

The men who create power make an indispensable contribution to the Nation's greatness, but the men who question power make a contribution just as indispensable, especially when that questioning is disinterested, for they determine whether we use power or power uses us."

- John F. Kennedy

There is power in questioning, so it makes sense that power itself should be constantly questioned. Questioning is proof of our own power and symptomatic of our liberation. When we bring others into powerful relationships, we invite them to question with us. So, the power we build with others and apply to purposeful work is only strengthened by being constantly questioned. This entire book, in fact, is in many ways a summary of my questioning of power to date; power in my work, in others' work, and in my life. If you take one thing away from reading this book I hope it is a new awareness of the role of power in our lives, an awareness turned vigilance, and one rooted in questioning what we think we see and know of ourselves and the world. Once we start to recognize what power is and where and how we experience and deploy it, we cannot help ourselves from probing more deeply into our relationship with it. Once we know power as a dynamic, not as a fact or a person or an institution, we can own it as a tool of our relationships and work.

Thanks for reading and sharing your power with me and for allowing me to share mine with you.

Don't forget to check out *Creating Matters: Reflections on Art, Business, and Life (so far)* and keep up with my blog at **www.andersonwwilliams.com**.

If you have ideas, feedback, or further thoughts to share, please feel free to email me at:

andersonwwilliams@gmail.com

Made in the USA
Columbia, SC
03 July 2017